T0279058

Writing in Color

Writing in Color

FOURTEEN WRITERS ON THE LESSONS WE'VE LEARNED

Edited by *Nafiza Azad* and *Melody Simpson*

JULIE C. DAO • CHLOE GONG • JOAN HE

KOSOKO JACKSON • ADIBA JAIGIRDAR

DARCIE LITTLE BADGER • YAMILE SAIED MÉNDEZ • AXIE OH

LAURA POHL • CINDY PON • KARUNA RIAZI

GAIL D. VILLANUEVA • JULIAN WINTERS • KAT ZHANG

MARGARET K. McELDERRY BOOKS

New York London Toronto Sydney New Delhi

MARGARET K. McELDERRY BOOKS
An imprint of Simon & Schuster Children's Publishing Division
1230 Avenue of the Americas, New York, New York 10020
This is a work of nonfiction. It reflects the contributors' present recollections of their respective past experiences.

For information about special discounts for bulk purchases, please contact Simon & Schuster Special Sales at 1-866-506-1949 or business@simonandschuster.com.
The Simon & Schuster Speakers Bureau can bring authors to your live event. For more information or to book an event, contact the Simon & Schuster Speakers Bureau at 1-866-248-3049 or visit our website at www.simonspeakers.com.
Interior design by Irene Metaxatos
The text for this book was set in Excelsior LT Std.
Manufactured in the United States of America

10 9 8 7 6 5 4 3
CIP data for this book is available from the Library of Congress.
ISBN 9781665925648
ISBN 9781665925662 (ebook)

TO ALL ASPIRING WRITERS. YOUR STORY IS IMPORTANT.
DON'T LET ANYONE EVER TELL YOU OTHERWISE.
—N. A.

THIS IS FOR YOU. YES, YOU. HAPPY WRITING.
—M. S.

Contents

Part Two
Journey: Querying, Publishing, and Beyond

101

Writing
in
Color

Nafiza's Note

My earliest memories of stories come wrapped in a voice that was as gentle as it was deep. The voice belonged to a relative who looked after me when I was a child and my mother was away teaching. The stories this relative told made me think, made me dream, allowed me to see the fantastical world shifting and roiling underneath the surface of the one I lived in. I am no longer a child, and the relative has passed away, but the stories she told me remain. They flicker within me, butterfly wings searching for release. I write so these stories can flow to someone else so that, just like I did when I was a child, they, too, can catch glimpses of the marvelous and wonder, *What if?*

When I initially conceived the idea for *Writing in Color*, I was certain such a book already existed. Surely, I thought, someone would have seen that aspiring writers in marginalized communities need visible reassurance that people like us, like them, have succeeded in the same dream they are working towards. Imagine my surprise when I found out that, though books aimed at aspiring authors are plentiful, there are few, if any, that specially address writers of color.

This anthology is certainly not exclusively for writers of color, but the essays do focus, in part, on how each contributing author's identity as a writer of color may have, in some way, shaped their experiences as creators.

In my journey to becoming a published author, I was told more than once by teachers that I have no aptitude for writing and should think about doing something else. It felt like the writing world was an exclusive club and I had been denied entry. My experience is not uncommon. For reasons unknown, the very people who are supposed to encourage you and ensure you don't give up very often become the obstacles you need to overcome to succeed.

When the language you want to tell stories in is not the language you were born in, you will be made to feel as if your right to this language is suspect. Perhaps the world will make you feel this way or perhaps it will be you who make yourself feel this way. I know I did and, in fact, a lot of times, I still do. Then I remind myself that coming to this language from a longer distance than those native to it is not necessarily a negative thing. This distance is also an opportunity to translate the beauty you see in a way that is uniquely yours. You can dress your stories in this language differently from others because you approach it from a direction in which others do not commonly travel. One of the essays in this anthology beautifully articulates the struggles of writing in a language and to an audience that are not, directly, your own.

Choosing to write stories is an act of courage for people who have been historically silenced. Choosing to raise your voice, owning the fact that you have opinions that may be against what the majority believe in, trying to assert your existence in a crowd of people most determined not to give you the dignity of one, are all acts of bravery. Stories are never just stories; they don't exist in a vacuum. Stories, for whatever purpose they are told, originate from lived experiences and sincere hope for a still amorphous future.

The essays contained within are about perseverance, translating the vibrancy of your culture into words and being scared while doing so. They are about dealing with jealousy and the roller coaster of emotions that comes with being an author. Some discuss writing for the individual when you come from a society that values the collective more, about learning the beauty of your brown skin through the stories you choose to tell.

These essays will hopefully accompany you, dear reader and writer, as you take that first step and commit the first word to the empty page. They will assure you that you're not alone in this journey. Yes, writing is a solitary venture, but your book is one voice in what is a conversation full of many voices. I hope these essays both inspire and comfort you as they did me.

Melody's Note

After you've attended writing conferences and workshops, after you've pored over books on the craft of writing, after you've listened to podcast after podcast and read interview after interview with your favorite authors, after you've gone on research trips, whether that be to the library or somewhere a plane takes you, how does your writing change?

After you've queried, after you've toured, after you've earned out, appeared on *Good Morning America*, and gotten your adaptation option, what words do you see on the page?

Do you see the rules and conventions of mainstream culture and society? Do you still sit down to write for yourself? Or do you suffocate on the smoke and let the mirrors cut through your feet?

The publishing industry hardens you. That's what you'll see in these pages. Imposter syndrome, a fraudulent feeling that boils down to being conditioned into not taking pride in your work, not properly acknowledging your success, worth, and well standing in your industry. People will ask you about how this affects you on panels and in interviews in the hope that they can put you in glass cages. Rejection, that people will say isn't personal when it clearly is because there can only be one and you are not what they have in mind. In case no one has told you, you can reject, too. Reject the bias, the racism, the colorism, the whitewashing, the microaggressions, the straight white cisgender American norm. You are already defined and no one can take that away. So write your words, and if you need encouragement, you can read these words too.

In these pages, you'll see a way through. Affirmation that it's okay to not conform. To keep the character names you want, to build the rich, colorful, and diverse world you are in love with in your imagination. You'll see that it's okay to demand to not be ignored. It's okay to pursue your goals and be just as shameless as anyone else pursuing theirs. It's okay to strive to be your best self despite the roadblocks society has set out for us. You'll learn from the writers who came before, from the writers who rejected defeat and have been through many storms to get where they are. And they are. Here. And so are you.

Throughout your writing journey, you'll come across a lot of writing advice that doesn't take into consideration your marginalized existence. You'll have to discern a lot for yourself, by yourself, but you are most definitely not alone. And you shouldn't be. So here we are.

There are a lot of books on the market about the craft of writing. But what comes after that and in between that?

How do you navigate all that comes with this writing career as a marginalized author? How do you navigate through jealousy? Through questioning from your own community? Through book bans? Through people who are not your allies but are your fans? How do you carry only what you need to unpack in your writing and nothing more? How do you define what your writing career success means to you while keeping all of the roadblocks in mind?

It's about time we get to discuss all of this and more. What an honor it is to be able to have read every single essay within the pages of this book. These writers have poured their hearts out in these pieces. I hope that each and every essay is as meaningful and impactful for you and your writing journey as it has been for me. Nafiza and I gathered this brilliant group of writers during a pandemic, a time that has, for countless reasons, been especially difficult for marginalized humans. I hope that these words, inked in love and loss, give you hope and clarity and infinite reasons to challenge people to see outside of black and white because you chose to write in color.

Part One

CRAFT
Starting from a Blank Page

Picking an Idea to Focus On

BY KOSOKO JACKSON

Kosoko Jackson is an author of young adult and adult stories that star queer Black men. His love for fiction came from writing his first story at age six about a pair of first graders who got eaten by a bear—his parents thought he had a problem. He most definitely does. When not writing, Kosoko is binge-watching cinema (he sees over one hundred movies a year), playing with his new golden retriever puppy, or suffering from existential ennui.

The Origins of a Writer

I always knew I wanted to be a writer. From a young age, words came to me easily and stories, mostly those that were fantastical and weird and strange, were where I found my safe haven. I loved to be that weird kid who spent his hours plotting and planning stories. I ENJOYED the thrill of coming up with a new world, making friends and characters, and putting them in situations that challenged them. Their struggles were my struggles, and my struggles were their struggles.

As a lonely Black kid who didn't have many friends, the first story I ever wrote was about three kids who went into a bear's cave and got eaten. I was an odd six-year-old. The second one was pretty much a rip-off of *Spy Kids* called *Adventure Kids*, but I wrote it on a PalmPilot, and I loved that story—all sixty pages of it. Next came *Dino Rage*, about kids who lived with dinosaurs and had to survive molten lava. Think The Floor Is Lava, but with dinosaurs.

When I was fifteen, I wrote an "epic" that was just three hundred pages of fantasy world-building called *Tear*. If you're an anime fan, think *Magic Knight Rayearth* meets *Final Fantasy*. It was a fun story; I'm not going to lie. That was the first massive novel I wrote. Was it good? No. Did it suck? Absolutely, but was it mine? Yes. It was my world, my struggles, my characters.

It was also the first story of mine with a gay character.

This might seem a little rambly, but it's important to understand where I started. Why? you may ask. Why do the works of a writer that never got published or even turned into full novels matter? If I can't read them, what is the point?

If you're a writer, you have a slush pile, your own version of one. Stories that you never finished. Stories you never edited. Scraps that you only got one page down on. All of those, especially the ones that came before you were published, or agented, make up who you are. They are your origin story, the pieces that came together that made you who you are. But you might be wondering, How do I, as I become a better writer, prevent that slush pile from growing bigger, and only focus on works I know will be successful?

Spoiler: that won't happen. You'll always have false starts. But what we can do, what I hope I can do, is help you have less of them.

Some of you reading this essay jumped into books and changed ideas because you couldn't get the voice. Some lost interest. Some sold a book in one genre and thought you couldn't write in another genre. I'm sure there are dozens of other stories too, dozens of experiences, sad songs, and happy tales about the stories you write, the stories you want to write, and the stories you have written.

I'm here to tell you, you're more than your ideas. The big ones, the small ones, the incomplete ones, and the complete ones. You're a writer, through and through, and that's a powerful thing. No matter what stage you're at.

But, Kosoko, you may ask. That's all good and shit but how about you actually get to the point, without rambling for twenty pages?

Fair, reader. Fair. But to understand the steps it takes to pick a story, it's important to understand one key thing: deciding what to write on is hard. You need to pick something that you're confident you can invest hours upon hours of your life in. Writing a book, at least a first draft, can easily take between sixty and two hundred hours (give or take). This number can change depending on how much time you can set aside to the art of writing, how fast a writer you are, and much, much more.

Be honest with yourself. Can you say, looking at whatever idea is in front of you, that you want to spend two hundred hours on it, writing one draft? And then another one hundred to two hundred hours editing, marketing, honing the book?

If the answer is yes, then good for you! You're further along than most people are.

But, if the answer is no, then the idea isn't for you. Not yet at least. And that's where these six steps can come in.

And that's okay. So many ideas start as shiny, fresh, new ideas, and when you put pen to paper, you realize you can't actually write them. This is normal; very, very normal.

When it comes to deciding what book to write first, I like to use this six-step decision tree to decide which idea is right to write. The key to this decision tree is to be completely honest with yourself. There's no point in lying or pretending like you're further along than you are. This is only to help you. You don't need to share this with anyone else, so why not put your best foot forward by being the most honest version of yourself possible?

Again, you need to find an idea that you love enough to write on to spend two hundred–plus hours on, but also something that you think will sell. Writing for yourself, and writing just for the art of it, is a beautiful and honorable thing to do. I will never tell you otherwise, and anyone who does is elitist. But, if you're reading this book of essays, you want to learn how to take your writing to the next level. We might have started writing for ourselves, but we evolved to wanting to write to share our words with the world; and to do that, we have to sell them.

There is a famous quote that I live by: "Write drunk, edit sober." I use that quote a lot when I'm coming up with story ideas and when I'm deciding on a book, but I modify it.

Write for your heart, write for the art, but edit for the business. Remember: writing for the business doesn't mean that you're losing the creative side; it just means your growth as a writer will help guide you to the next level of your career.

Question One: What Am I Contracted to Write?

What are your responsibilities? If you are a writer who has already sold a book, then you might have something called an option clause that you need to keep in mind. An option clause means that your publishing house already has a first-look requirement for your next work. These sorts of clauses can be restrictive, or they can be incredibly open-ended, but if you have one, then that probably means you already sold one piece of work. That means, in general, you're going to want to write something that aligns with your previous work to keep your audience engaged.

If you don't have an option clause, or if you haven't sold a book yet, this answer is a little bit more open-ended, and in that case can be a little bit more daunting. Don't worry, I'm here to help you.

In general, the first thing I always like to ask myself is, What do you have to write? Is it because you promised it to your agent? Is it because you promised it to your editor? Or is it some other contractual reason that has come up that means this idea has to get done? Did you enter a pitch contest and are agents awaiting your edits on a book? Is there a certain buzz around something that you tweeted that has gotten editors and agents chomping at the bit? If you answered yes to any of these questions, then that is the idea that you need to focus on—and that's a good thing! You have industry interest, something that's hard to get.

Here's the thing, reader. Something that people don't tell you is that writing is not a meritocracy. Those who are good don't always succeed. Luck, as with most creative fields, plays a big role in what books get published. So, when there is a spotlight on you because of something that you did with some ties, it's important to take advantage of it. That spotlight may never come around again.

Question Two: What Fuels Me?

Good news! You don't have anything under contract, so you're free to write whatever you want. The world is literally your oyster. There is freedom in that, trust me.

Remember how earlier on I said to write what you want, and edit for the business? Just like in high school, when you learned that you can have negative numbers, when before we were taught that numbers can't go below zero . . .

This is just like that.

Yes, you should write what you want, and you should always edit it towards the business, but you shouldn't lose sight of what makes your eyes light up. Writing is hard enough as it is when you're trying to hit deadlines and also trying to ignore reader expectations or critiques in your head. You should make sure that what you're writing is first and foremost for you.

What I mean by this is that your writing should always have a piece of you inside of it. Maybe it's a side character that you incredibly enjoy, or there is an idea or topic you want to tackle that is integral to you as a person. No matter what it is, there should be something about a book that makes you excited and tells you, this is your story to tell, or the story you want to tell. You're not going to always love every piece of the book, and you might write something and realize, 90 percent of the way through, you're just doing it for a check, or to keep your name active.

Reader, this is not a bad thing. We too often, as artists, think art has to always come first. But when your art becomes a business, that's not always a luxury you can have.

Writing, at this stage, is a business, and I think it's really important that you ingrain that in your brain. There's going to be a time when you're only writing for that exact purpose. And there are going to be times when you're writing because the story is something that you love so much, you just have to get it down on paper and share it with the world. It would be great if each time you put pen to paper, these two sides of you were in perfect unison, but it's more often that they're not. Don't let that dull the shine of writing for you. So, if you don't have to write what's under a contract, and you're staring at a blank piece of paper and trying to decide what to write, then start with that question.

What fuels you?

Question Three: What Do I Want to Be Known For?

Many authors have a theme. Be it a genre or a specific trope that they like to explore. And many authors expand outside of that, but most authors, at least for their first two or three books, follow a specific type of theme throughout all of their stories.

Angie Thomas writes (for now!) Contemporary Black Girl empowerment stories. Adam Silvera started with science fiction. Hannah Whitten is serving us folkloric horror.

Generally, I like to ask myself, What do I want to be

known for? For me as a writer, all of my stories focus on the empowerment of queer Black characters. So, this means, no matter the genre, this theme is something that finds its way into all of my stories. That allows me to write in any genre I want, as long as my "brand"—stories that empower queer Black teens—stays true.

There are advantages and disadvantages to not having a specific genre that you write in. The advantage is obvious—you get to jump around and write what interests you the most. But the disadvantage is that you're not building a strong following in the same way someone who writes within the same genre is. In some ways, it kind of feels like with every book of mine, I'm trying to build my genre base all over again with there being some rollover from the previous books simply because I'm building a general fan base.

So, when trying to decide what type of book to write, you should think about what type of writer you want to be. How does the story play into that? Are you known for something online or already in the universe that you want to capitalize on? Are you trying to create a world that is vastly different from what you normally inhabit? Deciding this will help narrow down your book ideas and help take your writing to the next level.

It should also be known that the type of writer that you want to be can always change. Another quote I like to think of is one that says, "Do not let a promise that you made to yourself ten years ago dictate your life now and prevent you from experiencing life-changing opportunities." Most writers are not the same people they were when they first started writing; as you change, so will your writing. That means if you're interested in something different now, then give that a try.

Question Four: What Do I Want to Learn?

This is kind of a personal one. Whenever I start a new book, I'm always trying to push myself to learn something new. When I wrote my debut novel, *Yesterday Is History*, I wanted to focus on how to write two different timelines successfully as a precursor to learning how to write dual-perspective stories. When I wrote my second young adult novel, *Survive the Dome*, I knew I wanted to focus on writing an action-packed thriller with good pacing. When I wrote my adult debut, *I'm So (Not) Over You*, I knew that I wanted to write a story that was a rom-com and focus on my romantic beats.

For me, it's a real joy to learn something within my own writing journey. I find I enjoy the writing the most, and I'm most proud of it, when I tackle a new skill and begin to master it within the story. So, at this stage, about halfway through deciding what book I want to write, I try to figure out which story would be the most challenging and what I'll learn from it.

But, reader, there's a trick.

The funny thing about this step is that sometimes I don't follow it, and that's as valuable as engaging with it. I know. Shocker! Sometimes it's clear which story is going to teach me the most, but because of time constraints or just energy, I pick the easier of the two stories.

But no matter the story, it's always important for me to

know what I'm learning from it. Even if I pick the easier story, that teaches me something internally. Maybe what I'm taught is that I'm approaching burnout. Maybe I want to jump into a different genre. Maybe the characters I'm exploring aren't the right type of characters for me anymore.

All of these lessons are important to know as a writer, especially burnout. Learning to pull back, to know when you need a rest and need to fill the creative well. In the end, I like to think that writers write stories not only to get an idea out into the world, but also to leave the world a better place than how it was when they entered it. And part of that sometimes means teaching yourself something.

Reader, even if a story resonates with no one, even if the story doesn't get published, if you challenge yourself, then you're on the way to becoming a better writer. Every writer will tell you each story that they finish makes them stronger than the story before. Which usually means ideas that you had when you were younger can now be tackled in ways that they couldn't be tackled before. Or the new ideas that come out of the woodwork are ten times more impressive, more fantastical, more relatable than the stories that you wrote before. This happens not because you hit the *New York Times* bestseller list, but because you challenge yourself and you grow.

Question Five: How Much Time Do I Have?

Time is not an endless resource. We like to think that we have as much time as we need in the day to get everything done and that our lives are going to be infinitely long. It's true that careers are long, but you have to be honest with yourself. And if you want to be a full-time author, reader, time management and honesty are key parts of that.

There are only so many books you can write. Even if being an author is all you want to be in order to become a well-rounded human, there are so many things you must do in the day, in the month, and in the year. To be a good writer, you also need to read. You also need to, if possible, find ways to insert yourself in the world to understand people's different points of views and lived experiences. To me, the best writers are those who find ways to explore the world, be it through books or be it through real-life experiences, or through movies. That takes time.

Reader, whenever you are going to write a story, it's important that you understand how much time you can put into it, and how much time you have. This isn't the same as just writing the story. There's time and energy that goes into plotting, getting to know your characters, understanding your characters, understanding the beats. Writing is only one part of creating a story; thinking is part two. So, when looking at your life and trying to understand which one of these remaining three stories you can write, it's important to understand how much of yourself and of your life you can dedicate to that outside of just pen-to-paper time.

Here's a hint: there really is no right answer here. Like I said, we are more than just people churning our stories. We have real lives, too. And it's important we include that living time in our writing process.

Question Six:
Am I Proud of the Story I'm Planning to Write?

Before I put pen to paper, once I finally narrow it down to the story that I want to write, I always ask myself the last and final question: Am I proud of this story?

The thing about writing is that you can't guarantee success. Even if your book sells to a publisher, there's no guarantee anyone will buy it. There's also no guarantee that any agent or editor will buy your next book, no matter what your success rate has been before. As I said earlier, writing is not a meritocracy. Publishing looks at each book as its own commodity, and their choices are influenced by past sales and current trends. The most important question they ask is: Does this product have the potential to sell? It's possible you could put whole years' worth of work into a book, and no one would want it.

You have to make sure that no matter what happens, you are proud of the book. Being proud of your book, and ingraining that into your mind, will also help you write through the tough waves of writing, because, reader, there always will be tough waves. If you're proud of the story, from beginning to end, no matter the outcome, the pain of it not being a success won't hurt as much as long as you put your all into the story and told the story you wanted to tell. Yes, each book is something that you put a piece of your soul into, but you'll have more books. What's more important is that you learn healthy coping mechanisms for when things in publishing don't go your way, and things in publishing will most certainly not go your way.

So, there you have it. These six questions are the ones that I used to guide my career every step of the way. Now, of course, as I mentioned in question four, you don't need to always answer these questions. Sometimes situations will come when the answer is clear, or sometimes you just really want to write a specific story. All of that is valid. These six questions are guidelines to help you when you do not know where to go.

I mentioned it earlier, but careers are long. In many ways, publishing is forgiving in ways other careers are not. You have the time to make mistakes, and more importantly, you're never too old and it's never too late to start writing. You could write a book when you're twenty and then not write another book until you're thirty. You can write your first book at fifty. You could start writing at twenty and write a book every year. All these paths are the right paths because different people walk different paths. Whatever path works for you is the path that works for you. Don't let anyone, including me, tell you what or how you should write.

Also, remember, writing should be fun. No job is always fun, no, and there are times when you want nothing but to give up, or start a new story. It's not uncommon to find yourself in a place where you hate your writing for weeks or months, but in the end, when all's said and done, and we put away the books for the very last time, we should look back on our career and not only be proud of it but say that we had fun doing it.

That is the most important question of all. Did you have

fun? Because if you did, then you did the right thing.

Here's the thing, reader. Writing is a hard journey, especially if you're a marginalized author. You're going to face a lot of challenges, people who don't get your work, who don't understand what you're trying to do, or who don't think your voice matters. But I'm here to tell you it does. It really, really does. Not only for those out there who read your stories, but for yourself.

So, keep writing, keep editing, keep dreaming, because one day those dreams will come true. But you have to be your strongest advocate, stronger than anyone else.

I know you can do it, and I'll be cheering for you from the sidelines. Now get back to work—you have a story to tell.

Writing in Color

A Unique Point of View

BY AXIE OH

Axie Oh is the New York Times *bestselling author of* The Girl Who Fell Beneath the Sea, XOXO, *and the Rebel Seoul series. Born in New York City and raised in New Jersey, she studied Korean history and creative writing as an undergrad at the University of California San Diego and holds an MFA in Writing for Young People from Lesley University.*

I was told "no" *a lot* at the start of my career, and countless times since then. So many writers have—*truly, one doesn't* feel *like a writer until one has been rejected a few times*—and yet, there's something about a "no" that can feel deeply personal to a writer of color. For one, oftentimes writers of color pull from their own background for their work, and so that closeness to the story means there's less of a barrier between the rejection and the heart. And, if you're anything like me—a voracious reader with a keen interest in the publishing industry—you not only notice the books that *are* being published, but also the ones that are not. This essay will hopefully be a warmhearted reminder that stories by writers of color are not only necessary, but wanted, and, through ruminating on my own career and process, give practical advice and heaps of validation.

Amidst querying what would become my debut, *Rebel Seoul*, a YA sci-fi action novel inspired by anime and Korean history, I was informed multiple times from agents that my book was one of many in a "saturated" market of dystopian novels. As a self-described reasonable person, I could understand, in theory, where these comments were coming from, as this was the age of *The Hunger Games*, and the resulting proliferation of novels with a similar plotline. However, what was frustrating to me was that a saturation of *Hunger Games*-esque stories meant my book set in a futuristic Seoul, South Korea, with giant mecha hadn't a chance. It was also disheartening to be grouped in this way, as I had never, up until that point, read a YA dystopian novel with Asian protagonists, let alone those who shared my Korean heritage. Later discourse from authors of color brought this exact topic to the forefront, along with a healthy discussion about how certain genres published in excess by white authors shouldn't have their doors closed before writers of color got their chance.

Luckily, Tu Books, an imprint of Lee & Low Books focusing exclusively on diverse novels for children, selected *Rebel Seoul* for publication. It was during the launch for that novel when I received a review with a turn of phrase that really struck a chord with me. The reviewer said that with this novel, I presented my own unique point of view. I thought this was such an interesting phrase, and it put into words something that had been percolating at the back of my mind for some time. Why, even when I received those nos or felt that odd, uncomfortable feeling that publishing didn't prioritize stories from people who looked like me, I never gave up on my dream of publishing my stories. It's because I believed I had a unique point of view.

And so do you. Everyone has a unique point of view,

and if you're a person of color, that is even more true about you in the context of publishing because our stories have historically been kept from the table and therefore we must make up for lost time. If we were given the same prompt to describe a door and where it leads, none of us would have the same answer. My door is hidden in a deep underwater palace, within a mural of a dragon clutching a pearl in one enormous claw, and pressing upon the pearl opens the door into a secret garden where a boy-god sleeps beside a pond of paper boats. What does your door look like? Where does it lead? Only you, with your background and experiences, your worldview and values, your interests and passions, hold the key to that particular door. How empowering is it to know that only you can write the story you want to tell?

Publishing has made strides since *Rebel Seoul* first released, thanks to so many smart people making noise and demanding their seats at the table. I can name quite a few dystopian sci-fi novels by writers of color, even those with giant robots (still not saturated, though, unfortunately). The table that once seemed so small and square turned out to be a magical table that grows as the need arises.

I Actually Got My Start in Narrative Nonfiction.

I don't know if I could have accepted the honor of contributing to this anthology if I hadn't gotten a bit older and published a few more books. Not to say I was any less qualified when I was younger. I respect all my past ages — sixteen-year-old me in particular was full of deep feelings — but there is a way in which age and experience make you care less about whether you have a right to say things. I'm definitely closer in age to those adults I respected when I was younger, and that also helps. I don't think that "imposter syndrome," in which one doubts whether they deserve recognition for their work, goes away, at least not for me, but it does help when the subject matter is my own experiences. I can feel confident that I at least know myself the best and therefore, in talking about my experiences, can give a true accounting of things.

I actually got my start in narrative nonfiction, which is like a college essay, if you've ever written one of those. Basically, it's a storied version of your life. I must have written a ton of them when I was in college, but I can recall distinctly having written three: one about the first time I saw my younger sister after she was born, one about punching a girl on the playground, and one about a boy I had a crush on whom I would only see during the summers. That's a picture book, a middle grade, and a YA novel right there! I mention these stories, and the fact that I started writing narrative nonfiction before I wrote fiction, because they made clear to me early on that putting lived experiences into a story was something I could do, and that it was rewarding! The concept was already there in the experience—it was about executing the story in a fun and engaging way. More importantly, it mattered to me. There were real feelings associated with those memories, and revisiting them in narrative form was emotional, cathartic, a balm to my soul.

When I talk about narrative nonfiction, I'm not talking about a word-for-word recounting of an experience, but a dramatization of it. Take the story about punching the girl on the playground, for example. This occurrence happened when I was five, and I have no memory of it. My mother was the one who told me about it years later. Turns out this girl was making fun of my brother because she claimed he was the worst player on the Little League baseball team, which I took extreme offense to. (I know this intrinsically even without having any recollection of it.) And so, when I wrote the piece, I was writing it from a lens of story, which means it had the setting of the playground of an elementary school, characters of the girl and me, and a plot with a problem to solve: defending the honor of my older brother! It might not have been a true accounting in the specific details, but it was true in spirit. Also, it ended with a great punch line.

This is how I approach my works of fiction, as well. In fiction, pulling from lived experiences does not make the work in any way autobiographical. It provides a starting point or inspiration for what specific details to include in a scene. In my most recent contemporary work, *XOXO*, about a Korean American girl who falls for a K-pop idol, I drew a lot of inspiration from my own experiences as a Korean American. In one scene, the mother of Jenny, my heroine, comes home to the small apartment the two of them share. In order to convey that feeling of "home" to the reader, I describe Jenny's mother taking off her shoes at the door and putting on a pair of house slippers. I describe the sweeping sound the slippers make as her mother moves across the kitchen floor to the rice cooker, which whistles as it lets out steam, a sign that the rice is almost finished. These are all sights and sounds that I've experienced in my own home, and through these descriptions, I convey what "home" is for my heroine. It's not just in my contemporary novels that I draw from the well of my lived experiences, but also for my fantasy and sci-fi novels. I included a hotel in *Rebel Seoul* that is based off a real hotel in Seoul, though I added descriptive elements to fit the sci-fi genre; in fact, I "futurized"—is that a word?—many real buildings and places in Seoul so that the reader might truly feel as if they were in an alternate universe, futuristic version of South Korea's capital city. For *The Girl Who Fell Beneath the Sea*, I distinctly decided to feature the Korean magpie in the story after a visit to the UN Memorial Cemetery in Busan, South Korea, where I saw magpies flitting cheerfully among the graves. They brought me such joy and peace, and had such a mischievous way about them, I had to include them in some way. It is through observation and small moments like this that I build my stories piece by piece.

There's this wonderful diagram called the cultural iceberg model, which uses an iceberg as an analogy to show the levels of understanding culture: the level above water and the level below the surface. On the surface level are the visible aspects of culture: food, clothing, holidays, and traditions. While below the surface are the aspects of culture that aren't as visible, like worldview, heritage, and family values. This diagram is the perfect example of why, when it comes to stories that center a specific culture, it's necessary to have those people who share that culture telling those stories. Only they will understand all the elements beneath the surface, for they live and experience those elements firsthand.

As I say this, I want to include two caveats. Although I believe taking inspiration from one's life can be a powerful tool, no one is owed another person's life experiences, especially if the experience is one of trauma. Secondly, writers of color should never feel they must be pigeonholed into writing about their own culture. I felt this pressure heavily when I first started writing, mostly because I'm stubborn and I always want to do the exact opposite of what someone tells me to do. A white professor in college told me I should think about writing stories for Asian Americans after graduation. I remember being very offended because I thought she meant that as an Asian American, I could only write immigrant stories, or stories that heavily featured Korean culture. It felt limiting to me when what I wanted to write were romantic fantasies and dystopias. It was some time before I realized that I could write romantic fantasies and dystopias with characters who looked like me, which is what I wanted to do all along. I just didn't know that was an option, as there were no examples of such stories when I was growing up. As writers of color, no matter what, our worldviews, inherently influenced by our cultures, will make their way into our stories, whether we're writing a story about vampires or space. I think it's truly a gift, and the innumerous stories by writers of color, each with their own unique point of view, give me a feeling of hope. I'm a writer, but I was a reader first, and the idea of that is incredibly exciting.

Where Do I Get My Ideas?

So many of us writers are first and foremost readers—that's what got us into writing in the first place. And quite a few of us can pinpoint certain books that we read as young people that began that journey into becoming a writer. For me, that book was Antoine de Saint-Exupéry's *The Little Prince*. Although I'd always been a voracious reader, reading *The Little Prince* was the first time I felt, beyond enjoyment of the story, as if I were engaging with the text on a deeper level. The passages became quotes I wanted to remember. I began to search for that feeling of emotional resonance and intellectual engagement in other books. When that wasn't enough, I turned to my own writing. I started tabbing books, a process I highly recommend to writers, in which I use colorful index tabs to mark passages. I mark passages with a conscious effort to learn from other writers, in order to improve my craft, but also to get inspiration and ideas for my own work. What do I mean by this? Let's take *The Girl Who Fell Beneath the Sea*, for example, which was partly inspired by my love of fairy-tale retellings I read and loved in my childhood, like Robin McKinley's *Beauty*, a retelling of *Beauty and the Beast*, or Juliet Marillier's *Wildwood Dancing*, which combined several fairy tales in a historical fantasy setting. Those books laid the groundwork for *my* retelling, as I wanted to write in this same tradition but where the original tale was drawn from my heritage. Similarly, I gained the confidence to write *Rebel Seoul* after reading Cindy Pon's short story "Blue Skies" in the anthology *Diverse Energies*, a story set in a futuristic Taipei, which would later become a full-length novel in *Want*. Before then, I'd never read a YA sci-fi with Asian protagonists, and her story changed my worldview entirely. I owe so much of my storytelling to the storytelling of others, and I'm proud of that. I don't think any book or writer exists alone. We're all in conversation with one another. We're in conversation with the books that came before us, as well as with our peers, and the writers who will come after.

For a person of color, the idea of engaging with previously published titles is more complicated, as classic novels (those that have historically been taught in schools, at least in the US—which is my frame of reference) predominantly center Western writers and experiences. It might seem incredible that I didn't know Asian people could be the protagonists of YA novels before reading Cindy Pon's novels, but before that lightbulb moment, my worldview was limited to Western classics taught in school and the YA novels shelved at my local bookstores and libraries, all of which featured mostly white protagonists. I found Asian protagonists in immigrant stories and works in translation but never in the commercial YA fiction that I loved so much. Which is why I personally found a lot of my storytelling touchstones outside of books, in anime and Korean dramas. Manga has had a huge boom lately, but when I was growing up, media out of Asia was very much relegated to the margins of popular culture. I found comfort in these stories that centered people who looked like me, told from creators who shared similar cultural touchstones. In the past few years, things have changed drastically in this regard, but I think this sentiment remains, of searching for those books or media touchstones that you find resonant, and the "center" is what you make it. In recent times I've loved pitches that compare things to popular anime or books published in the past decade.

When coming up with story ideas, I often ask myself, What would I like to read? Sometimes it's about finding that gap on the bookshelf and filling it, or reading something and thinking, I could do a similar thing but through my unique point of view, making it fresh once more. I've come up with story ideas in all different kinds of ways. *Rebel Seoul* began as a dream, the details of which never made it into the book, but it gave me such a strong feeling of yearning, which stayed with me throughout the whole writing of that novel. I've written whole books because of a song (*Rogue Heart*) and because of an image that stayed with me (*The Floating World*). There is no wrong or right inspiration for a book. Perhaps you want to write a spin on a Western classic. Perhaps you want to write a spin on an Eastern classic. The true test is whether the story means something to you, if it's big enough to become a part of your personality—because during the writing of it, and the publishing of it, it does become a part of your personality. When writing the book, you talk about it with your family and friends, you share snippets with critique partners— other writers with whom you exchange work in order to give and receive feedback—perhaps even with strangers, and then once it's published, you promote it online and at book events. So while writing your book, ask yourself, Is this book unabashedly me? If the answer is yes, then I think you're on the right track.

Not to say every story has to be etched from your soul—I just think you should care about it a little. Personally, the more I care about a project, the more excited I am to work on it! The more a project reminds me of other things I love, the more I'm excited to work on it too. Recently, before starting a project, I've taken time to gather things that remind me of the project. They can be physical things, like books or candles or music albums or boards pinned with clippings from pages I've torn from magazines, or they can be intangible things, like saved images on my computer. Then, as I write, I pick up those objects and return to those images, and I'm inspired.

I write as if the book is already a story waiting to be told. As if it will fit right among those other books I've plucked from the shelf. To me, that's the secret of writing: believing your stories should and need to be told and that you have every right to be here.

Stet, Intentional

BY CHLOE GONG

Chloe Gong is the #1 New York Times
bestselling author of These Violent Delights
and its sequel, Our Violent Ends. *She is
a recent graduate of the University of
Pennsylvania, where she double-majored in
English and international relations. Born
in Shanghai and raised in Auckland, New
Zealand, Chloe is now located in New York
pretending to be a real adult.*

There was a moment a few years back when I became incredibly aware of where my tongue naturally rested inside my mouth. Now that I've mentioned this, you're probably thinking about your tongue too—about whether it lies at the bottom of your mouth or floats right in the middle or presses behind your front teeth. And if you've been on the internet for long enough, maybe you've seen the same fun fact that sent me into a tongue crisis: that your native language determines where your tongue is most likely to rest, and English speakers will have their tongue near the top. Whether accurate or not, the fun fact did give me pause to wonder what my tongue was supposed to be doing if I spoke two native languages that have completely opposite sounds. Did this pseudoscience account for the diaspora? If there was a general rule that said the sounds of English meant I was more likely to press my tongue against the roof of my mouth, was my tongue inclined to do its own silly little thing inside my mouth if it was native to too many sounds?

I started asking my friends where their tongues rested

inside their mouths. I got enough varying answers that if I were the one conducting a scientific study, I'd probably conclude that a tongue's resting spot is more dependent on how big someone's mouth is rather than the language they speak . . . so it probably wasn't too scientific, really. All the same, I was fascinated by this idea that there might be certain rules associated with your physical voice, so it's hardly a surprise that it led to some pondering about the rules associated with having a writing "voice" too—how the way we construct fiction is supposed to follow conventions and structures passed down from the books that came first. Follow the rules: everyone who speaks English has their tongue pressed to the roof of their mouth, so rest your tongue at the roof of your mouth to pronounce the best English-y sounds. Follow the rules: everyone who writes novels in English commits to a certain set of expectations, so make sure to do that as well if you also want to tell stories with narrative flair and long-lasting cultural impact.

"You've swapped point of view three times within two paragraphs," a friend pointed out while reading an early draft of my debut novel.

"Is there something confusing about it?" I replied. I was ready to adjust and edit to make sure everything made sense, so I needed to know where the issue had popped up. "Did I label a dialogue tag wrong?"

"Well, no." A pause—or what I imagined to be a pause when we were typing into a chat box. "I just thought that wasn't allowed."

The most common writing advice always surrounds

what we are and are not allowed to do. There's this idea that one most correct way to write exists, and if you perfect that one way and never scribble outside the lines, you're going to produce the world's greatest work of art. To an extent, of course rules exist for a reason. They are guidelines, like training wheels on a bicycle so that someone first starting out doesn't completely topple over and fall before they have scarcely completed one lap around the park. But imagine keeping your training wheels on when you're pumping up a steep mountain competing in a triathlon. They would only be restrictive, because you've long learned how to ride in a straight line, and now you're doing everything in your power to ride fast or ride strategically. Writing rules in the English-writing community say we shouldn't switch points of view willy-nilly unless there are section breaks or chapter breaks because it will be confusing. It is important that a reader stays in the head of the character, that they aren't jarred out of the narration and flung from perspective to perspective before they've fully secured their understanding of the scene. All of this is true. I suppose over time, rules have gotten shortened and their nuance shaved off the sides, because a warning that should say, *Be careful how your point-of-view perspectives change in case it invites confusion,* has turned into *Do not switch points of view between paragraphs at all or else you're a terrible writer and no one is going to want to read your book, also you should probably just delete Microsoft Word permanently.*

It's essential for every writer to realize that "rules" come with a long history of actually being guidelines, suited most for newer storytellers trying to find their footing. But just like people who—by the parameters of pseudoscience—have a tongue that doesn't rest anywhere, this is particularly tough for writers of color who are influenced by a cultural background different from the English-speaking majority and, as a result, build their worlds in different ways. I have always wondered why I instinctively utilize rapid third-person point of view, switching when I want to shake a reader to pay attention. I had long decided that it was fine if I broke the rules: there was no long, angsty process of wondering if I needed to delete my entire book, because I had been writing for so long that I understood why the rule originally existed and I understood what I was doing when I made the active choice not to follow it. In the traditional publishing process, there's a fun little word called "stet," which means *let it stand*. I understand it as an instruction that basically means, *Hey, I see what you tried to fix here, but that's okay, I liked it the way it was before.* I love *stet* because it feels powerful. At once, editing is a necessary process that will make your book stronger and stronger, and it's a process that pulls you through the wringer to make you consider what you are and aren't willing to stand by in your book. What has been done intentionally? What has been defied with purpose in an effort to make a certain narrative choice, and what was actually just a weaker mistake that slipped in? *Stet* is that differentiation tool between rules that were accidentally broken and rules that were broken with intention and decision. When someone points to something funny I've done and I see that it genuinely reads strangely, I make a change to tidy it up. When someone points to something funny I've done and I can mostly justify why I did it, then *stet, intentional!* goes into the comment reply box. I almost wish that existing as a writer of color was as easy as just typing in those two words to the world, but the truth is, sometimes justifying your choices is really hard, especially when you first start out. I don't think I would have known how to verbalize what I was doing earlier in my writing career; I was mostly feeling around and telling stories in the way that felt natural to me. If I kept tracing and tracing, the way that my brain digests the English language begins on a whole different wavelength.

Shockingly, I only read translated Chinese literature for the first time in college. (It was Ding Ling's stories, in case anyone is wondering.) Suddenly, I was spotting third-person point of view–switching everywhere, the text flitting from one character to the next without the classic section breaks that are standard in the books I've always grown up reading in English. Still, it wasn't as though I could argue that I was originally influenced in that manner. It wasn't as though I'd grown up reading these translated texts and that was what I mimicked when developing my writing style. But culture is hard to define. The background we are raised in and the guiding hand of intergenerational style permeates into the very way we think. In retrospect, I should have thought: *Of course.* I speak an entirely different language, I was told stories as a child from this language, I follow traditions and community practices that are entirely separate from the

Western world. Why *wouldn't* I draw from that experience to develop my writing style? Why *wouldn't* my voice end up different from the norm, different from the majority who are a part of another culture?

"I'm really enjoying these short stories," I told my mum on the phone, midway through that semester. "I feel like I'm understanding the way you think."

She laughed, but it wasn't an exaggeration. Reading translated literature created from my parents' culture puts reason and voice behind matters that I would have just thought are the way things are. It makes someone think hard about history, and intergenerational trauma, and customs and patterns that pass onward and onward. Then I thought: What does the literature *I* create reveal? How many other children of my exact diaspora can I reach with these ideas and, maybe for the first time, reach through the page and make a moment of connection to show a reader that there are others out there who feel what they feel and think how they think?

"I'm a five-act-structure kind of writer," I was telling another friend, later in the revision process when I was splitting my one cramped manuscript into two books and trying to understand how the sequence of events would change without the whole thing falling apart. "I don't even think that's a cultural thing. Shakespeare wrote plays in five acts. No one gets more classic Western white man than Shakespeare."

"Even if you're pulling inspiration from Shakespeare,"

the chat box said, with more typos, "the three-act structure is all the rage these days. Anything that goes against it is rebellious by the standards of this decade's craft books." That was fair enough: Shakespeare was writing for an audience four hundred years ago. It isn't the same anymore. "Maybe you watched more slice-of-life epics than hero's-journey arcs while growing up. Maybe that's where it comes from."

I hummed my agreement to myself, but it wasn't as if I could do an exact count on the number of movies I'd watched in my childhood: draw up one column predominantly for Western-influenced action-adventures and another column predominantly filled with Studio Ghibli whimsy-filled narratives. I barely even remember most of those films I consumed while growing up—I only remember being parked in front of them anytime I visited my grandparents, given a can of coconut milk to drink. Yet stories emerge in the missing gaps, in the memories of half-realized blurs and dreamlike shapes taking root while the details float away. The narratives that call to us will come with their own set of conventions and expectations. Some slower stories expect an act structure more staggered than the norm. Some ideas expect a tone more distant than the norm. If you stand by it, then it's not *wrong*, it's just different, and you plant your feet in with each *stet, intentional, let my writing voice have a funky tongue position!*

Even before I really dug into the source of my writing style, I knew it was important to internalize that not every book is for everyone and there will be readers who like your work and readers who hate your work—that's just how the world goes, no matter what. That being said, I thought it wild that, at large, it has been decided that certain features of how I write are deemed to run against the grain. The way I perceive the world, digest it, and present it forward is deemed to run against the grain; some part of my creative work will end up being a rule breaker, one way or another. On the flip side, someone who has only consumed the dominant culture, someone who is only influenced by the dominant culture, will find it natural to follow the rules. Of course they will—they have been constructed and molded by these rules to begin with, after all, and they will produce storytelling that has been deemed good and excellent and with such great understanding of writing rules. The rest of us have to prove ourselves. We have to issue statements that say, "Don't worry, I understand how craft works," and essays about our intentional subversions to urge the reading community to remember that there is not one standard of story, and the belief that there is stems from Western hegemony. I'm an author of traditional publishing, after all. It doesn't matter how much I'm aiming to first and foremost reach that little circle of fellow Chinese diaspora readers who are my primary audience. There are other circles I need to think about: general readers who I want to touch too and would love if they also adore my books. Because we continue getting published if the sales keep coming in, and isn't that mighty difficult if we're already predisposed to be incomprehensible? Each time we sit down, we think hard about each *stet*, because that could

Writing in Color

be the difference between someone nodding along to your story and someone tossing the book aside because they've decided that you don't understand the rules of English grammar.

So where do we—writers who draw from cultures different from the majority—go from here? Before we can balance the struggle of writing authentically inspired by our background and writing that is accessible to the larger Western audience . . . How do we even identify which facets of our writing are genuinely in need of improvement and which facets of our writing aren't *bad*, they just don't adhere to the rules that the cultural majority are used to? In the same way that some of us will run against the rules, I also don't think there is one solution that will be a Band-Aid for everyone. For some, maybe finding early readers who come from similar backgrounds will help identify what genuinely doesn't work and what is only a matter of cultural literacy. For others, maybe you can only really go for it and write however you want until you develop strong writing by trial and error. It's hard not being able to offer a solution after pointing out an existing problem, but to begin with, not enough writers of color are even aware that we start at a different point and we have to claw our way out with ten times more self-confidence than non–rule breakers. If you look at your work any differently after this, let it be with a more generous eye. Only you know where your tongue is *supposed* to be resting when you're speaking in your natural cadence. Your craft, too, is the unique tone you take with the world. No matter what the majority are trying to press toward you, as you develop your writing, the most important thing you can remember is that intentionality is key, and if you have closely analyzed why you would defend your *stet*, then you are allowed to let it stand.

Untold Rebellions: Character Agency through the Lens of Collectivism

BY JOAN HE

Joan He is a Chinese American writer. At a young age, she received classical instruction in oil painting before discovering that storytelling was her favorite form of expression. She studied psychology and East Asian languages and civilizations at the University of Pennsylvania and currently splits her time between Philadelphia and Chicago. She is the New York Times *bestselling author of* Descendant of the Crane, The Ones We're Meant to Find, *and* Strike the Zither, *the first in a fantasy duology.*

People want autonomy. Emotional independence. The right to privacy. In the West, these are axioms. After all, what are the alternatives? Mind control? Emotional codependence? Constant surveillance?

What if I were to tell you that half of the world doesn't prioritize the three values I first listed? That there are people who'd put in-group harmony over personal preferences and see emotional dependence as a strength rather than a flaw? People who would give up their privacy if it meant a safer society? What would you think?

Would it sound dystopic to you?

The Hunger Games was my gateway book. As in, it was the book that really got me into young adult. Prior to it, I'd read *Maximum Ride*, *Twilight*, and whole library shelves of paranormals. I'd read everything from *City of Bones* to Sarah Dessen. Even earlier, I'd read *How I Live Now*; to this day, I think of it as an iconic example of the teenage voice. But it was *The Hunger Games* that really sucked me into

YA and made me want to contribute my own stories to it.

I've wondered why. So many elements from the book stay with me to this day, from the exploration of media and entertainment in an authoritarian state to the wide-ranging effects of war. But the most vivid moment I remember falling into the age category came at the end of chapter one, when Katniss volunteers to fight to the death in place of her sister, Prim.

In the years since, there's been an outpouring of YA that focuses on sibling relationships. I've written one myself. But when *The Hunger Games* unveiled its inciting incident, I wasn't thinking about sisters at all. I was thinking about how this was the first time I'd personally encountered such an opening act of sacrifice in young adult. I was thinking about father-daughter relationships.

I was thinking about Mulan.

I have a theory as to why Disney picked Mulan, out of a plethora of Chinese legends, to adapt for its Western audience. And that theory has nothing to do with Mulan's homeland popularity, but everything to do with its titular character and her very obvious agency.

Let's take a moment to agree that agency, in its simplest definition, is when a character affects the plot. A character's choices must push and shape scene after scene; the narrative exists *because* of them. If you were to remove the character from the plot and insert someone else, would the story still unfurl like it did before? If not, then the character you removed has agency.

Writing in Color

But here's the rub: you can write a character who fits this definition of agency, and yet they might not slot neatly into what agency often looks like to a Western YA audience. That's because several biases are baked into this concept of "agency"—biases that aren't necessary to agency at all, but rather give it a more familiar and recognizable flavoring.

One such bias is for that of **defiant** agency.

Defiance is relative, of course. In a society that sleeps all day, for example, something as small as waking up can be viewed as a huge act of defiance. This raises a point that I want to drill in: the environment of a character, and how much they do or do not conform to it, inform not if they *have* agency, but rather how much their agency is highlighted, is spotlighted, stands out like a black sheep— pick your term. Point is, this initial framing sets the stage and lighting for any future acts of the character. It's the prologue that gives us a taste of what to expect; we'll talk about the epilogue later.

This is why I think the legend of Mulan, fundamentally, even without the bells and whistles Disney later added, works so well for a Western audience. Not only does its inciting incident feature a great act of agency from Mulan, but she also acts in secrecy, suggesting a level of defiance against her parents and societal norms of the era. This defiance dovetails nicely with Western ideals of independence and, since we're talking about stories, the gold standard of a coming-of-age tale that usually culminates with forging a path for yourself. The journey can start with the motivation of saving another person, or toppling a dictatorship, or remaking the future. That's not the important thing. The important thing in this kind of story is that it's you, the individual, against the world. The world might not change for anyone else, but it'll change for you, because you're exceptional. Different from the pack (remember: defiance). Your actions are power.

Your wants matter.

Want. Action stems from it. You want something; therefore you act on it.

Right?

Here's a false dichotomy—knowing what you want, and not knowing what you want. It's much more complex than that, a fact that popular Western writing craft books do acknowledge. Sometimes, the thing you want isn't the thing you need. The character simply hasn't realized what it is they need yet, at the start of the story. And so much of the growth that takes place in a Western coming-of-age tale is about bridging that disconnect. A character learns more about what they truly need; their actions are more powerful as a result.

However, what if you know very well what you want? But you don't act on it? What if you act on the wants held by the people around you? What if you don't act at all— you let the world burn, let the people die—because the friction between what you want and what others want is too great? Does that mean you have less agency? Does doing something simply for approval, or not doing some-

Writing in Color

thing because of the promised disapproval, reduce your agency?

One point of view would lead you to believe yes.

Let me share mine.

My parents immigrated to the US from China when they were in their early thirties. They knew no one here, had no safety net to fall back on. They uprooted their lives so that I could lead a better one. Their sacrifice weighed on my mind as early as childhood. In middle school, I knew very clearly what my parents wanted my future to look like. Of course, I had my own opinions too. But a part of me was always reminded that it was a privilege to be in a position to daydream. To have personal preferences. To have choice.

Much of what my parents preferred didn't matter when they were my age. My dad's goals were simple, and universal: to survive so that he could take care of his parents one day. His childhood took place against the backdrop of the Great Famine preceding China's Cultural Revolution. Later on, as he tried to become one of the first in his rural village to go to college, his actions stemmed again from one simple, hardly unique motivation. It wasn't necessarily that he *wanted* to study English, but he had to. And when he failed the college entrance examination year after year (to this day, it's still offered only once a year), he knew he had to keep on studying not because he wanted to, but because the alternative, facing the shame of his village and family, was simply unacceptable.

The stakes of my adolescence weren't nearly as life-or-death. But every action I took, I also thought about in the greater context. If I were to write a contemporary novel featuring myself as the main character, I'd probably be dinged for having no agency. There would be no rebellion—not on the outside at least. Crushes existed; all went unacted upon. When I quit art—my biggest act of defiance, since my parents had believed in my talent—I funneled the extra time into studying for college exams. I didn't want to do well on them, in the way a main character wants something; I wanted to do well because I had to. I got in to—and picked—the college that I knew my parents could be proud of to have on their tongues when they phoned our relatives back in China. That mattered to me much more than any personal identification I had with the college in particular, be it its school spirit or its programs. I *wanted* to do what my parents wanted.

I wanted to thank them.

I knew what my parents wanted; I also knew very clearly what my own wants were. I quit art because another art form was calling to me: that of the written story. In the interludes of this contemporary story of my life, I was writing. I was querying. I say "interludes," because again, this didn't map onto the main plot. This story doesn't culminate with me majoring in creative writing or surprising my parents with a book deal or anything like that. As a matter of fact, while committing to my major of psychology, I was well aware of my parents' wants for me still (a PhD in the field). But everything I'd done up until this point was to figure out when I would start acting for myself.

And that time had come.

In essence, my coming-of-age story revolved less around learning about myself and more around learning about the people and systems around me, and my relationships with them. By the end of my journey, I knew that I'd done enough to feel like I'd repaid my parents. I wouldn't have regrets. This end was my beginning, and this story would not have the shape that it does if not for my particular choices and actions (or lack thereof). Insert another character, and the journey might start earlier or later. But just because the structure of the story is different doesn't mean there isn't a story. It's my story, and I made it because I had agency.

Now bear in mind, my home environment did not mirror that of the country surrounding me, one founded on individualistic principles. Whatever values I hold have been molded by my particular upbringing and whatever culture my parents passed to me, and those values won't be a carbon copy of someone raised within a predominantly collectivist society.

Which begs the question: What do "individualist" and "collectivist" even mean? As terms, they've been bandied about for decades in social psychology circles, and countless papers have been written about the two camps of cultural values. As with everything, there's much more nuance than "cultures of individualism value the individual" and "cultures of collectivism value the collective." But to spare you a lecture, we're going to boil it down as much as possible.

Individualistic cultures emphasize the inherent separateness of traits and goals from person to person. Collectivistic cultures view people not through what makes them unique as individuals but through their relationships with others and their place in society. In studies[1], people from more collectivistic countries were more likely to describe themselves in terms of interpersonal relationships (I'm a daughter, I'm a student), whereas people from individualistic countries described themselves more in terms of innate traits (I'm kind, I'm stubborn). When the bilingual subjects were presented the survey in the language of their collectivist culture, they described themselves in more collectivist terms, and vice versa. The takeaway? Culture—and language—shapes thought. Thought shapes want, and want, notably, is the impetus behind which actions we choose to take, if any. In short, culture flavors character agency.

Certainly, not every person from a collectivist society will always choose the more collectivistic way of thinking. But even that added awareness that you're breaking away from the cultural norm introduces a wrinkle to your thought process before every action you take. Too many wrinkles, and the characters risk reading old. Write a character with conventional agency—they know what they want and are taking action for it—and you might just see capability conflated with maturity. The way your character considers the consequences of their moves on the circles

---

1 https://as.nyu.edu/content/dam/nyu-as/psychology/documents/facultypublications/jimuleman/Rhee1995.pdf

Writing in Color

around them makes them seem not teen, if viewed through the lens of a society that doesn't understand such considerations as second nature, but rather the product of prefrontal cortex development. Their actions might be defiant, but this brings us to the second bias: Western YA wants agency, but with the spirit of recklessness.

I want to challenge that. Maturity does not necessarily mean more emotional or mental control. Maturity, in a culture that values harmony with the in-group, can mean thinking for yourself. Maturity can be unlearning the sayings that are drilled into you as a child—the nail that sticks out is hammered down—and realizing they're not applicable to every situation. Maturity can mean growing a little more reckless. If maturity in an individualistic culture means doing more of the conscientious brainwork to think of how your actions affect the circles around you, then who is to say that maturity doesn't move in the opposite direction for a more collectivistic culture?

I want to bring us back to *The Hunger Games* for a moment. Katniss's goal—to protect her sister, Prim—could be considered a collectivistic goal. After all, in that moment when she volunteers, she's not thinking of herself as "the good hunter" or "the one who hates the Capitol," but in terms of an interpersonal relationship: she is Prim's sister.

As a sister, she ought to volunteer.

Now, I can't say that *THG* was the reason, but given that publishing is a business that makes profit-driven decisions, it must not be total coincidence that we've seen much more normalization of these collectivist self-descriptors and motivations in YA literature in the years since. However, it's worth noting that these kinds of familial relationship–focused stories for teenagers have existed for a long time in other cultures and aren't as groundbreaking as Disney's *Frozen* would have you believe. Ironically, the very framing of a character as different/exceptional because they care about their sibling and not, say, a romantic relationship is leaning into an individualistic mindset that values uniqueness.

Furthermore, it's clear that despite more characters enjoying "collectivistic" motivators, the same expansion has not been granted to how we view agency, with a certain kind being deemed "exciting" and "teen." How, then, can you write a character who's influenced by the collectivistic mindset, but who can also be pushed through the publishing gates and onto shelves?

Let's return to the layers surrounding agency: we know there's the driving want (with a bias toward wants that are different from what others want). You have the decisions characters make in pursuit of those wants (with a bias toward a reckless heart). And finally, you have the consequences of that agency. What happens in the story as a result of the character's thoughts, actions, or behaviors? Is the agency rewarded or punished?

If breaking out as your own person is a rite of passage encouraged by the culture, then one might imagine that we'd have a lot of stories rewarding agency and framing it as a good, desirable thing. But in a collectivist society,

Writing in Color

that's not always the case, and it's in the outcomes that I personally have been able to push my own little envelope the most. Because to an extent, by nature of storytelling, you want to write about the characters who are different, versus the average Joe. You want to write about the character who has a fierce want—whether it's right for them or not—and who pursues it boldly. Maybe a character doggedly pursues their goals. And maybe they succeed. Or maybe they fail. Maybe the effects of those actions ripple beyond their immediate family, catalyzing consequences they didn't think of—not due to recklessness, but because it's a lot to recognize how small you are in the world. Action comes with great reward—and great risk. Who knows how the dice will fall? By leaning into the uncertainty, I can allow my characters the sort of agency that feels familiar to the audience without placing a cultural value judgment on it.

One of my favorite storytelling devices is to close a book by mirroring how it opened. So as we're nearing the close of this essay, wherein I've chucked a lot of craft-talk at you, I want to take you along with me on a case study between two *Mulan*s. One is the 2009 film released in China, directed by Jingle Ma and starring Zhao Wei and Chen Kun. The other is Disney's 1998 rendition. Through this, I hope it becomes clear how the culture from which a story is born—and the culture it is then adapted to—changes not only world details and character attitudes, but how agency is framed.

Before we start, I want to acknowledge that the *Mulan* Disney produced is intended for children, whereas China's 2009 *Mulan* war-action film is more PG-13. However, there's no reason to believe that China's 2009 Mulan isn't a young adult, considering she's still unmarried in an era when most married young. Conversely, the marriage and war plotlines of the Disney edition are much more "young adult" than one might expect from the Mouse. With that disclaimer, let's begin.

Both Disney's and China's *Mulan*s are based on "The Ballad of Mulan," a poem that documents Mulan's replacement of her father; the twelve years she spends in the army during the Northern Wei period of China, fighting; and her ultimate return home, upon which she reveals to her fellow soldiers that she's a woman. This is the source material; both Disney and the 2009 Chinese film have taken liberties with it, one perhaps more so than the other.

I've emphasized the importance of framing the agency as defiant or expected, especially at the "prologue" or beginning. We'll start by analyzing Disney's *Mulan*. The original ballad never mentions anything about Mulan being on the cusp of an arranged marriage. Disney, however, drills in on that as one of the opening songs, "Honor to Us All," establishes what is expected of Mulan by her society, peers, and family, and how Mulan chafes against those expectations. There's an obvious discordance between how she really feels on the inside and how she must present herself. Her act of agency at the start, therefore, not only serves to protect her father but also sets her on an individualistic journey of fulfilling herself as a person, unique and separate from the women around her. There are parallels to *THG* here too—even though Katniss performs her initial sacrifice in a burst of altruism, one cannot deny that her character was repressed prior to this act of agency. She's been catching game, but it's forbidden; she's under the thumb of an oppressive system that would execute her if they found out what she was doing. Though the Games are just as oppressive, in them Katniss is able to capitalize on her personal traits and skill sets. She also learns more about herself—what her strengths are, and her weaknesses. Every moment of agency furthers her development in such a way that she's set further and further apart from her peers and home, back in District 12.

There is no such opening framing in the 2009 *Mulan* film; we do not linger on the repressiveness of the society. We do not get any sense that Mulan yearns for something more than what her surroundings or family can give her. From a YA craft standpoint, one might argue that this is a lack of character depth. But consider it from a different angle: it might simply be true to Mulan's character, the way this story wanted to tell it. Again, defiance is not a necessary part of character agency; Mulan can just as well volunteer in the war. Her personal reason is the one that starts and ends with her relationship to her father, and her role in this society, as a daughter. Volunteering is what she ought to do. And just because she ought to doesn't mean that every character in her situation would.

It's one thing to know what's expected of you; it's another to actually have the guts to follow through.

As you can imagine from such a prologue, in the 2009 film Mulan's enlistment is a much quieter moment, devoid of thunder and lightning. *But it is still agency.* For without this act, the rest of the story following the events of the war would not unfurl. And unfurl they do, in both renditions of the tale. In Disney's *Mulan*, they defeat the antagonists and save China. The emperor personally recognizes Mulan as a hero. Mulan goes home, and what a world of difference her agency has made! Framed directly as a result of her defiant choices and actions, the family that awaits her is suddenly much more open-minded than the one that she'd left. They welcome Shang in as the love interest, and no arranged marriage is spoken of. *Agency is rewarded.*

At the end of China's 2009 *Mulan*, Mulan also returns home victorious—it's by her cunning and bravery that she leads her troops to prevail over the enemy. Again, this is agency; even if another daughter *had* been as dutiful and had had the guts, they might not have had the sensibilities and smarts that Mulan had to succeed. But when Mulan returns from the war, she returns to the role of being a daughter. Just like in the source ballad, while much has happened as a direct result of her actions, enough to fill legends to come, the surroundings and values that shaped her remain the same. The soldier she meets and falls in love with while in the army is decreed by the emperor to enter a diplomatic marriage. The love interest asks Mulan to run away with him, and perhaps in a different telling of

Writing in Color

the narrative, colored by a different lens, Mulan, having defied once, would realize that she wants to defy again. She would say yes.

But in this narrative, Mulan declines, saying that they should choose to serve their countries. The movie closes with the sense that nothing around Mulan has really changed. And that is exactly what she wanted when she volunteered in the place of her father: to preserve her family and society. She fought out of duty and loyalty. She remains aware of the bigger forces around her and abides by them, because that's what her culture values. That doesn't mean it's easy; when she gives up on selfish, individualistic love, you can feel how much more difficult the choice has become after all that she's been through. But in spite of the difficulty, her choice doesn't change.

Perhaps this ending strikes you as quite hollow. Perhaps it gives you the sense that Mulan doesn't have agency. But remember: the story has a shape, one that this Mulan directly carved. It might not be an uplifting, Disney-approved shape, but that's beside the point.

Now, I can already hear the rumblings. *Can an empowering story be told through a collectivist lens?* My counterargument is that going above and beyond to fulfill a duty for your family requires much more strength of character than most can muster. But I also understand the importance of meeting the individualistic storytellers and readers in the middle. So I'll leave you with this:

In the Disney version, Mulan is unconscious when a doctor finds out that she's a girl. Her identity isn't revealed by her own choice, though one can argue that the reveal is caused by an act of agency (pulling off a daring move on the front lines and being gravely injured as a result).

In China's 2009 film, Mulan successfully hides her identity from almost everyone within her battalion. She reveals it only to her enemies in an act of deception that ultimately defeats them. When she finally stands before the emperor, she reveals to him that she's a woman, on her own terms.

I'd say that's a pretty empowering moment.

No way of thinking of story, character, and agency is superior. They are simply different. Of course, the commercial-minded might argue that the Disney retelling of the ballad is "superior" because it clearly appeals to the audience that it's supposed to and follows the rhythms of story and agency that have been popularized in the West. But what is familiar and popular is not—and should not be—interchangeable with what is the gold standard. If those two things were really interchangeable, then the call for more stories from marginalized backgrounds would never have taken off. And as the call for diverse stories grows, that diversification should extend to that of craft, convention, and rhythm.

Axioms should instead be questions.

How does your character fit in their society? What do they feel about the systems and people around them? What are their wants, and do they act on them? Or do they act on the wants of others? What are the consequences of their actions? How do the people around them react? Does the character develop different wants? Does how people perceive them change as a result of their actions? Do they change the world?

They could.

Or they could not.

You, as the author, have agency.

You can choose the shape of your story.

And Then?

BY KAT ZHANG

Kat Zhang started dreaming of being an author when she was twelve years old. Said dreams didn't come to fruition until seven years later, when she sold her young adult trilogy to HarperCollins. Since then, she's written several middle-grade novels and a growing collection of picture books. When she isn't writing, she loves to travel, draw, and pet every dog she sees.

My parents filled my childhood with stories. When I say this, people imagine bedtimes cozied up with picture books, or daily chapters from children's classics. They think about *Goodnight Moon* and the Berenstain Bears and Harry Potter.

In reality, I remember my dad reading to me from only one book: a battered, blue copy of *The Complete Tales of Winnie-the-Pooh* (which also contained all of A. A. Milne's poems for children). It weighed at least five pounds. We'd curl around this encyclopedia-sized tome, learning together about Pooh Bear and Piglet and the Hundred Acre Wood.

The rest of my parents' stories came from memory. I listened to them during grocery-shopping trips, during excursions to the bank, during hour-long drives to and from my dad's work, where I sat during summer vacation, reading books and waiting for him to finish. These stories were mostly in Mandarin. Tales of Sun Wu Kong—the Monkey King—and his great battles against an endless stream of goblins and ghouls. Romances (with inevitably sad endings) where the lovers turned into butterflies or ended up separated because one of them was banished to the moon. True-to-life snippets from their childhoods in China.

My favorite stories starred San Mao, an impoverished orphan boy named for the three hairs on his otherwise bald head. He lived on the streets like Oliver Twist, surviving through wit and luck. I'd hang on to every word, anguished by every pause in the telling—and there were always so many pauses as my mother stopped to pay the cashier or my father bemoaned a missed exit on the highway.

"Ran hou ne?" I'd demand from the backseat. This is Mandarin for "And then?" and was my constant refrain during these fractured story times. "And then? And then?" In recent years, children's publishing has been just as eager for new stories, viewpoints, and cultures. Diverse voices are blooming, creating a landscape very different from the one I encountered a decade ago, when I published my first novel.

Fed this steady diet of stories, I soon aspired to write my own. I was seventeen when I started *What's Left of Me*, a book that became the first in a trilogy called the Hybrid Chronicles. By high school, I'd devoured the shelves of school and public libraries, so I was an expert in children's literature from a reader's point of view. And over the course of that literary education, I saw few signs anyone was interested in science-fiction featuring an Asian pro-tagonist. Consequently, I never considered giving *What's*

Left of Me a non-white lead, or including any aspect of the Chinese stories I'd grown up on.

The Hybrid Chronicles describe a world where everyone is born with two souls—two separate minds and personalities nestled inside one infant. They have their own voices, wants, and needs. They're even given separate names by their parents. But one soul usually disappears by the end of toddlerhood, leaving the remaining one to grow up in lone command of their body. In the Americas, a governmental entity spanning North and South America—and where the series takes place—this is the accepted natural order.

But some rare people never lose either soul. They share their body with their twin like siblings sharing a bedroom. These so-called hybrid are mistrusted by their communities, blamed for all sorts of societal ills.

What's Left of Me was only the second novel I ever finished. I was still in the early stages of figuring out how to structure a story, let alone a series or an allegory. But looking back on those books, I see how they reflect my teenaged ruminations on being a minority. About people fearing and maligning what they're unfamiliar with, and what they don't understand.

Writing the Hybrid Chronicles took me all the way through college. It's impossible for me to separate that first series from my university experience. I was growing as a writer, but even more than that, I was growing up. Publishing taught me so many lessons about perseverance, navigating the adult working world, and handling both successes and disappointments It showed me that achieving a dream is not an end point, but a continuing journey.

I turned in the third Hybrid Chronicles book right after graduation and was soon looking for a new story to tackle. Several false starts followed. Then my dad, freshly returned from a visit to China, told me an interesting news story he'd heard abroad: a legend about a long-dead Chinese emperor and hoards of ancient treasure. Finally, the story-making engine for my next book started turning in earnest.

For a long time, I'd wanted to write something inspired by my parents' stories—both the Chinese mythology and the true tales from their lives. But what? I'd toyed with the idea of historical fiction. Ancient China is a rich world to explore, and when I was growing up, there was little other than *Mulan* to introduce children to her. But I was worried about doing the research. Despite my parents' best efforts, I can't read much Chinese beyond my name. Certainly not enough to comb through primary sources.

Of course, there are lots of books about ancient China in English. But what would I miss if I limited myself to English-language sources? It's always a little sad to see the richness of my childhood stories reduced to a few paragraphs on Wikipedia. I'm bilingual and bicultural enough to know the nuance that gets lost in even the best translations. The turns of phrase that lose color without the right cultural background.

The past is already a foreign country, even to those who still live on the same land. How much more is lost in translation when one culture studies another's past? And writing historical fiction is about more than the facts, like what countries were warring and who was king at such and such time. Think of how much we learn about Western history through a lifetime of storybooks and movies. Never mind if it's historically accurate—it's a common backdrop, a starting point that we share.

Despite my worries, my dad's story wouldn't leave me. He'd been visiting my mom's family in Fujian, a province in southeastern China, when he heard about new interest in an ancient tomb. It had been discovered long ago, and for ages, everyone believed it was the final resting place of a Ming Dynasty monk. Now that idea was being called into question because of the stone dragons guarding the grave.

In ancient China, dragons were strongly associated with the emperor. They emblazoned his robes. They decorated his throne. A common man couldn't just carve a dragon over his doorway. So could these stone dragons mean something?

Perhaps not.

Or perhaps it could be a clue. A clue that this monk wasn't a monk after all.

Who, then, could it be?

The answer to *that* question, my dad said, was even more interesting.

More than six hundred years ago, during the Ming Dynasty, there was a young emperor named Zhu Yunwen. He only ruled for a few years before a jealous uncle murdered him for the crown. Supposedly. Some believe that the emperor didn't die. Instead, he escaped into the Fujian countryside disguised as a monk and lived out the rest of his days dreaming of retaking the throne. Knowing the funds he'd require for such a task, he hid a great treasure somewhere in the countryside . . . one that's never been found.

The more I thought about Zhu Yunwen's story, the more I wanted to commit it to paper. I wouldn't need to make the story historical fiction—his undiscovered treasure gave me the perfect way to tie past to present, to link the story of an ancient emperor with that of a modern girl.

Before long, I started drafting *The Emperor's Riddle*. In it, twelve-year-old Mia Chen embarks on a summer trip with her family to Fujian. She's most excited to spend the trip with her aunt Lin. Unlike the rest of their more practical family, Mia and Aunt Lin share a love for history and adventure. But Mia's plans are dashed when her aunt mysteriously disappears soon after arriving in China.

Her mom thinks Aunt Lin is just being flighty, but Mia is convinced otherwise. *She* thinks her aunt was kidnapped. It's too much of a coincidence that Aunt Lin disappeared right after discovering a treasure map. Mia sets out with her older brother to solve a series of puzzles that will hopefully lead them not only to Zhu Yunwen's legendary hoard but also to their beloved aunt.

Many parts of *The Emperor's Riddle* came easily. I'd visited Fujian often as a child, gorging on fresh seafood and getting caught in summer monsoons. I knew what her streets looked like. I also knew about awkward relationships with extended family members who feel like strangers. About the pressures of being a shy child torn between politely playing the role of niece or cousin—of family—and hiding in the guest room with a book. About the guilt that comes from these warring feelings.

Other parts of *Riddle* were inspired by my parents' lives. We're introduced to Emperor Zhu Yunwen and his mysterious treasure by Aunt Lin, who became obsessed with his story during the Down to the Countryside Movement. This was a period during the Chinese Cultural Revolution when millions of Chinese teenagers, freshly graduated from high school, traveled from the cities where they were born and raised to labor in the rural countryside. It lasted roughly a decade and encompassed my parents' generation.

My whole life, I've heard stories about their years away from home. Some are amusing (if terrifying), like the time my mother, wielding a scythe to cut grass, accidentally grabbed a green snake. Others are straight-up terrifying, like my father's memory of going down to the river to bathe in the dark, only to wake up with his bedsheets covered in blood and his skin covered with leeches.

Aunt Lin's experiences as a teenager during the Down to the Countryside Movement are a small but important part of *The Emperor's Riddle*. They ground the otherwise fantastical story about secret riddles and hidden clues—about shining treasure and dastardly plots—in a real-world context. Aunt Lin, stifled and bored during her time laboring in the fields, dreamed about Emperor Zhu Yunwen's treasure as a way to incite her imagination and pass the time. My parents told me of similar experiences. Both highly academic people, they hoped for the day they could go to university.

I have subtly (and not-so-subtly) suggested to my dad, who has expressed interest in writing novels, that he write a memoir—or at least a novel—about his childhood and young adulthood. He always brushes it off. But he and my mom were happy to talk with me when I wrote *The Emperor's Riddle*, acting as my primary sources for Aunt Lin's experiences.

The tricky thing with novel writing is that every new project feels like starting from scratch. All those great tools you learned from a prior book seem useless in the face of brand-new problems. The Hybrid Chronicles was a first-person, science-fiction, young adult series. *The Emperor's Riddle* was a third-person stand-alone middle grade that threw all sorts of new trials in my path. The fact that it was my first foray into a story involving China and Chinese culture only added to the challenge.

Some of my initial concerns turned out to be warranted. It *was* difficult to find a wealth of knowledge on Zhu Yunwen in English. Luckily, *Riddle* focuses on Mia's hunt for Zhu Yunwen's treasure, not Zhu Yunwen's life itself. Between my resources and my parents' patient help, I gathered enough research to write what I needed.

I also stressed a lot about whether or not I was doing my parents' stories justice. I feel a lot of responsibility when trying to tell someone else's history—even if it's history told through fiction. While I was lucky to have such willing and accessible interviewees, knowing that I was in part telling my *parents'* story definitely upped the ante. I

Writing in Color

didn't want to fall into the pitfall of overdramatizing an experience (even a very dramatic one) or oversimplifying it.

Of course, books are built on drama. Anyone who's ever seen a movie "based on a true story" knows that nine times out of ten, the "true story" had fewer car chases and gunfights and probably took place over three years, not three weeks. But at what point does overdramatizing a real experience veer into milking it for shock value?

I think about this in particular when creating stories based on the experiences of people that my readers may not be familiar with. I worry that overdramatizing is a way of othering. Of making life in another country—even if it's life in another country in a different time—seem so strange and incomprehensible that we can't imagine it ever happening to ourselves.

All stories must come to an end, both for the reader and the writer. After a lot of revisions and nail-biting, I sent *The Emperor's Riddle* to my editor for the last time and crossed my fingers that it would be well received. Not long afterward, I wrote *The Memory of Forgotten Things*, a foray back into science fiction that didn't touch on China at all. There's nothing like writing a new book to distract you from the release of a previous one!

But there were many parts of *Riddle*'s debut that were too happy to miss: the school visits where I got to share Zhu Yunwen's story and talk about Mia's adventures, the sweet notes from kids and librarians who enjoyed the book, the honor of the Parents' Choice Award and the NCTA Freeman Honorable Mention. The latter made me the proud author of "a book with a sticker on it," something which would have sent my child self into ecstasies.

Soon after *Memory*, I started drafting the Amy Wu picture book series. In writing *Riddle*, I'd come to realize how much I enjoyed illuminating parts of my childhood, tucking them between pages of a book where readers might stumble upon them and see themselves. As a child, I'd never lamented a lack of Asian characters. I'd taken it as a matter of course. But as an adult, I see the ways that lack of representation affected the way I saw myself and my place in the world. I'm thrilled that kids growing up today have more opportunities to find themselves in their stories.

Each Amy Wu book is inspired by a memory from my own life: *Amy Wu and the Perfect Bao* by the bao zi (little fluffy steamed buns) I used to make with my parents, *Amy Wu and the Patchwork Dragon* by a painting I created in elementary school, *Amy Wu and the Warm Welcome* by my experiences translating for Mandarin-speaking students in class, and so on.

But part of the magic of fiction is the ability to stretch beyond one's own life. I still dream about a novel set entirely in ancient China and look forward to the day when I can dedicate more time to research. In the meantime, I'm watching far too many Chinese historical television shows, which serve double duty as research and a way to shore up my Mandarin. (My parents appreciate the latter.) At the very least, I might gain the pop-culture familiarity with China's past that I have with Western history, growing up on a diet of knight-and-princess tales.

I'd also love to write a book based on Chinese myths. As every fantasy reader knows, there's something marvelous about a made-up world that feels fleshed out beyond the boundaries of the page. Introducing Chinese legends into a work primarily consumed by Western audiences can feel like a shortcut to creating this lived-in feel. And it's wonderful to share the rich stories I've grown up with. But again, there's the pressure to get things *right*.

My parents are amused by my dedication to the details of fables. "They're just stories," they say. "There isn't a right or wrong. Just make it however you want." I understand where they're coming from. After all, fairy tales are constantly molded and retold. How many reiterations of *Cinderella* have we seen? Of *Romeo and Juliet*? Of *Peter Pan*? The fun lies in changing the details, making the familiar new and exciting again.

But these are Western stories told to a Western audience. It feels different to add an allusion to the tale of the butterfly lovers, or a mention of Nezha, or to retell the story of Chang'e—but set in modern-day high school. This may be the first—it may be the *only*—time my reader will be exposed to these characters, this story.

In *Amy Wu and the Patchwork Dragon*, it's Amy's Asian-inspired dragon that first confuses her friends, then gives them the opportunity to learn about another culture. Fables may "only" be fiction, but what novelist doesn't believe in the importance of fiction? They are often our first exposure to peoples and situations outside our families. They can incite sympathy and curiosity—or mistrust and fear.

I am, of course, only one of an army of Asian authors publishing in children's literature. Every year, I see more books featuring Chinese characters. Some are historical fiction. Others are set in the modern day. There are romantic comedies and fantasies and mysteries. Each one I read teaches me more about writing sensitively and responsibly. Every day, there are new conversations about how to best tell a story about another culture.

Can there be foreign words that go untranslated? If there are, should they be italicized to signal to the reader that they are foreign? What if that doesn't ring true to the story and characters, who wouldn't see them as foreign? How should we write Asian names in English-language books? With the surname first, as they'd be depicted in their original country (especially if the book is set abroad), or in the Western convention? Should Chinese words be written syllable by syllable, to reflect how they're written in Chinese ("zuo zi" to mean "table"), or together, to reflect how they'd be seen as a single word in English ("zuozi")?

Clearly, I'm not the only one grappling with the best way to thread my family's culture and history through my work. How to be honest and respectful and truthful—while still telling an entertaining tale.

I would love to share more of the stories I grew up with. That were passed down to me brick by brick, building the foundation of my childhood. And as a second-generation Chinese American, I'll always struggle against certain barriers when it comes to learning about my family's original homeland—her fairy tales and culture and customs. But

Writing in Color

the labor of learning is a labor of love. There are so many more stories to learn, to try to understand, and to translate into my own writing.

I may be decades older now, but I am still that little girl in the backseat, in the line at the grocery store, at the bank, asking, "Ran hou ne?"

And then?

writing in your mother tongue

BY LAURA POHL

Laura Pohl is the New York Times *bestselling author of* The Grimrose Girls *and its sequel,* The Wicked Remain. *Her debut novel,* The Last 8, *won an International Latino Book Award in the YA fiction category. She likes writing messages in caps lock, never using autocorrect, and obsessing about Star Wars. She graduated from the University of São Paulo in literature, studying Brazilian masters, Greek and Latin classics, and an unhealthy number of Russian romances. This essay is her first published nonfiction work. A Brazilian at heart and soul, she makes her home in São Paulo.*

People will call you brave. You must get used to this.

They will mean it as a compliment. They will think it's endearing that you set out to write a story in a language that you weren't born speaking, that hasn't been ingrained in your mind the same way it has in theirs. They believe a language is something you are awarded, not a tool you've learned to wield, sharpening it like a sword so that it will fit your purpose; its blade sturdy, its edges cutting. They believe their language is complicated when you have learned to switch between yours, when you have learned to identify which parts come from different places, when all your word choices are deliberate.

Throughout the years since I've been published, many people have asked me why I decided to write in English. I am Brazilian; I live in Brazil; I have no plans of moving to the USA or to Europe or anywhere else people deem every inhabitant from the Global South must want to move to. There are many reasons why I started writing in another language, and many reasons why I continue to do so.

The first reason people think of is money, and that's absolutely true. The money does make a difference if you live in other parts of the world where your coin is devalued. I always find it amusing to see writers in the USA talk about how much money they (don't) get paid, and when I compare it to what writers get paid here, in my country, the difference is brutal. Most Brazilian writers don't even get an advance for their books. Most Brazilian writers do not get to make a career out of writing, even if they hold a day job, because the income from books is so meager that dedicating yourself to getting one book published is a herculean task, and a career requires that you do it continuously.

The second reason, the one that motivated me the most, is readership. There's a market for books in the USA that is infinitely bigger and more wide-reaching than the one in Brazil. It's more competitive—first you need an agent, and then a publisher—but there was always a chance, as small as it was. But even with the competition, it was a fair game, a game you can choose to enter. There will be rejections (personally, I garnered more than two hundred in three manuscripts before getting an offer from an agent), but more importantly, there will always be some amount of opportunity.

In Brazil, there are writers still fighting for recognition. We have imported books and movies and culture from the USA for so long that the consumers believe that if it's from our own country, it's automatically worse. We have an expression for it, coined by Brazilian playwright

Nelson Rodrigues: "síndrome do vira-lata," a collective inferiority complex when comparing Brazil's culture to other countries', especially in the Global North. It's rooted in racism, the idea that Brazil has no cultural refinement to distinguish itself amongst other nations. Back when I first started considering writing as a career, more than once I heard other readers scoff at books written by contemporary Brazilian writers, refusing to read them because they were mere imitations of the real thing, and many Brazilian publishers followed suit. The reasoning is simple: if it's gringo, it's better.

How could I compete with that? How could I ever make it to that standard?

There was only one way I could show everyone that my words mattered. That way was writing in English.

You will have to prove yourself. You will have to justify every word choice you ever make. People will think that they are arbitrary, that the words fluttered onto the page by magic, and that you have not spent the better part of your day crafting a single sentence. You will spend days, weeks, months, watching TV shows and movies and reading books and listening to podcasts, scraping every single one of your resources, because if you make a mistake, they'll blame it on you not being good enough.

You have to prove yourself twice and thrice better than your peers, because you must not let them think you don't understand them, that you don't speak the same language, that you are not just as good as they are. You cannot afford to even think of the sentence *What is the name for that?* or I *forgot what it's called*, lest the world think you're a fraud.

You will never learn how to spell "strengthen" correctly on the first try, but for all intents and purposes, you have learned the meaning of "veracity," "pejorative," and "irreverence." It doesn't matter that you knew these words before Americans learned them for their SATs, because they are words rooted in Latin, and in your language they are used by peddlers exchanging choice words about their merchandise. In your language, you are never in doubt, but you had to leave it behind because it wasn't the right one.

Most media consumed worldwide is standardized with English as the universal language. Anything *American*, especially, is considered universal. (And what *is* America, may I ask? It's an entire continent, but the only *Americans* people refer to when saying the word are the ones in the USA.) I've grown up reading about the International House of Pancakes, Twinkies, Pop-Tarts, the Super Bowl—things that don't exist or are irrelevant in my world. I know all twenty-six Brazilian states, sure, but I also know at least twenty-something of the American ones off the top of my head. Sometimes I can remember the names of American presidents more than I can remember Brazilian ones. (We haven't had as many, also thanks to American influence.)

It's impossible to live in a world, especially one deeply connected with the internet, without suffering the overwhelming interference of American culture. Without see-

Writing in Color

ing the American way as the standard, because they have worked hard to be the center of all media, with books, movies, and everything we consume. Everyone outside the USA's borders who works in art is familiar with their world, and even the misconceptions we have are based on the misconceptions Americans have about parts of their own country. People *expect* all of us to know these things. I can recite many things about American culture that I've learned, and I'm not even sure where or when I picked them up; I simply know it, have been exposed to this information all my life. I could also easily challenge people to tell me three things Brazil is known for, and you're not allowed to say *coffee*, *soccer*, or *monkeys*.

Why must we talk about this? Because it's important to realize that there was no need for me to cross worlds and barriers to write in English. I grew up watching Spielberg and Hitchcock. I listened to Beyoncé and Michael Jackson and Madonna on every radio station. I read Atwood and Fitzgerald and Riordan. There is a barrier, yes, and to the others, the keepers of language and arts, it'll appear insurmountable. For us, it's always going to be a transparent wall, and we've seen everything there is to see on the other side even when we've chosen to avert our eyes.

Personally, there was a deliberate choice for me, when I began writing novels in English. I meant to find an audience that would embrace my work more widely, and ironically, for that to happen, I couldn't write in my mother tongue. To have readers in France and Germany and China and Turkey and Australia, I'd have to write in a language that could unite them all, the one all these people regarded as their *second* language, the one we've all been subjugated by. But finding an audience there, finding success, meant that my work could also no longer be ignored by my own country. It meant that if I was good enough for the rest of the world, I was good enough for them. That *we* were good enough for the whole wide world.

That choice was also a watershed moment for my writing. I didn't only have to think of the final goal of publishing, but it permeated every single narrative choice I was making when writing. Who would be the protagonist I'd choose for my story? The setting? The conflict? I started writing in English in 2014, and the initiative of We Need Diverse Books had just been founded, and so much work has been done since then—but not at the time. To pursue it as a career, to make it worth my time, I was aware I couldn't afford to be *different* from the other American writers. I had to be like them, and blend into a category already filled to the brim.

To make it into a career, I had to ask myself: What was the line I wanted to draw between myself and my work? How much was I willing to do in order to make my publishing journey happen? Because there will be things to give up, every choice will demand an abdication. And in writing, I tried asking myself what in the work would appeal to *me*, while also appealing to everyone else who was going to read it. Because I came from another place, because my language was another, I had to assess what was worth investing my time in. I had a finite number of hours, and I had to decide how to make them count.

It's impossible to guess what publishing wants. It's impossible to determine beforehand which story a publisher will like but not connect with, which story will ring true but will lack development. It's impossible to predict what will sell—all those things are true. But it's also true that you can look at the market and what is being published now, what kind of stories people have always yearned for (white, straight, cis), and you can exploit it in the best way you can, the way you feel that will be best for you.

And thus, it's like setting up an overcomplicated jigsaw puzzle, one with far too many blue pieces of sky. To write, you must find your voice. To publish, you must have that je ne sais quoi in your writing. To continue in your career, you must appeal to an audience whose homes you've never been to, whose houses you've only ever looked at through Google Street View.

How do you tell a story that appeals to the whole wide world? How do you set someone up for that, and expect them not to fail?

You will feel, sometimes, that you have sold a part of yourself that no one will ever see again. You will feel that when you write, you have started to think like the people you're molding yourself into. You will feel that you have lost some integral part of who you are to become this. To be able to write like publishing wants you to write, to tell a story that is read as universal, to write in English as if you were born thinking it from the day you opened your eyes and heard the doctor's words confirming that you were breathing and living. There is a loss most writers don't speak about, because they can't understand it—you've spent so much time trying to think like they think, telling the stories they want to hear, that you're not sure you are entirely your own anymore.

When you write in your language, it doesn't feel like it's yours anymore.

When you tell your story, you don't feel like you have the right to tell it.

In 2018 there was an updated study on the diversity of children's literature, compiled with the data provided by the Cooperative Children's Book Center. According to the study, 10 percent of books feature African and African American protagonists, 7 percent feature Asian and Pacific Islander and Asian-Pacific protagonists, 5 percent feature Latinx, and 1 percent feature Indigenous and First Nations protagonists. Out of those, several are actually written by white writers. According to the study, overall, 50 percent of children's titles contain white protagonists, and the second largest group, 27 percent, feature animals. Lee & Low did a diversity baseline survey in 2019 about workers in the publishing industry, and with no surprise, considering all departments overall, 76 percent of workers are white.

There are no statistics for writers. I have no idea how many writers are writing with English as their second language, but considering the diversity above, I can't imagine it's more than 1 percent.

Marginalized writers, both of racial and queer back-

Writing in Color

grounds, already have it harder to break into the industry. And this presuming that they are writing in a language they know very well.

The point being that it's hard. I won't need to reinforce that. I'm sure you'll read all the essays in this book and think that it's hard, it's hard all the time. It is. Being recognized for your writing and making a career out of it takes years of practice, and it takes patience to face things that are beyond your control.

And it's so easy to forget yourself amidst the journey. To forget the why of what you're doing, and just focus on finally achieving that goal. I think it's a normal feeling for all writers, that once you get to your objective, you aren't even sure if the story you wanted to tell was worth it in the first place.

I felt this especially after publishing *The Last 8*, and more recently *The Grimrose Girls*. I was asked several times why I was writing those stories—a story about a Mexican American resident of the USA facing an alien apocalypse, and a story about four girls living in a boarding school in Switzerland, none of which are Latinx, Brazilian, or even remotely like me regarding the obvious aspects of my nationality and my experience—and I'm not sure I've ever been able to give this question a good answer. First: Why not? Second: these were the stories I was sure would find an audience where I was trying to sell them. American writers don't have to think about whether or not they're going to find an audience; they were born amidst their audience, they were born being part of it.

The so-called American dream is so ingrained into their thoughts that the mere belief that they can write a story means it will find the right audience, that they belong there if only they dare to dream.

Again, it returns to the question of the universality of a story. When you're trying to write a story to make money on it, to grow your career, it's hard not to think of the audience you're writing for. There's a lot of advice that floats around saying, "Write your story and don't worry about who's going to read it"—but once you're sitting down to actually make this real, it's almost impossible to ignore it. I wasn't someone sitting in a cutesy New York flat, watching the lights dance on the reflection of the windows. I wasn't the quirky writer putting a laptop in my bag and going to the nearby café, writing down the words as I sip a pumpkin spice latte. (What even is that, anyway?)

And even then, I still speak from a place of relative privilege. I am Latina to everyone in the United States and Europe, but still white in Brazil. Again there's an expectation and a label that comes from outside our experience, as foreign as we are to them. No one in Brazil says they're Latino, and the same goes for most of the other South and Central American populations. We're Latino because the USA needed a word to explain why some people didn't have the right background to set foot in their country, that they weren't the kind of americanos they wanted to welcome. Ask a Diaz in the USA what they are, they'll answer Latino; ask a Diaz in the other thirty-three countries of Latin America, they'll answer everything but. We're white,

Black, Asian, Indigenous, a mix of all of these, and our racial perceptions are entirely different from those in the USA. I've been asked more than once by Latino-focused events to provide content in Spanish, and the intent is to be inclusive and *diverse*, but even this kind of thing shows how different racial perception is inside the borders of the USA, and it's even more demeaning when it comes from people who you consider your allies. Latinos aren't a monolith. Brazil's language isn't even Spanish.

Only 1 percent of Brazil's population is fluent in English, according to the data researched in 2020 by the British Council and the research institute Data Popular. I am white and from a middle-class family, and my parents always emphasized that learning English could unlock doors for me. It did, but that also explains why many others don't travel the same path. In several other countries of the Global South, those statistics are even more abysmal.

In writing, you're always catering to an audience. That audience might be you, but the thing is, if you're American, there are probably other Americans who have the same interests as you, who have had the same upbringing, who will share the same stories, and to them, your story will make sense. I, being Brazilian, had to imagine an American audience to relate to, craft my story around people who I had never even met other than in the realm of the internet, based on the stories they told me all this time. It's a game of shadows, of making puppets on the wall, trying to reproduce something you feel is the right tone. I think I must have gotten at least a part of it right, because my books were published, and they have found an audience.

You will wonder: Did that part of me ever exist?

You will wonder: Was I ever anything else, other than what I am now?

You will wonder: Is English even my second language?

I started writing in Portuguese again. It was slow at first, a tentative dip in the metaphorical pool. I expected the water to be icy, but it was welcoming, like a daily bath at the end of a long day. The language was familiar and beautiful and exciting. I was writing a story only for myself.

And when writing, I realized that I didn't have to always succumb to expectations. Publishing will always try to make you *sell*, and that's not bad. After all, we all have to pay bills. You can find a balance between writing what they want to hear, and writing something that you love, a story that you want to tell. You can learn to sell it to them, feed them back what they always tried to feed you; you know them better than you know yourself. They have tried to conquer you with their books and movies and media, but all they ever did was give you weapons so you can conquer *them* instead. You know what they want. Take what you are owed.

In a way, I've also found the promise of the American dream, but I'm not so naive as to believe that I've gotten there because there's a land of opportunities. *Dreaming* is for the Americans; all of us others need feet on the ground

Writing in Color

and have work to do, and working has a price. I know what it cost me, and I know what it has given me in return. Even in publishing, you can't escape capitalism.

Since I started writing, it has gotten better. Publishers want to diversify (at the same time they are trying to limit everyone's work: "We already have one Black writer. Why would we need two?"), but your voice, your story, and your choices also make you unique. There will be times when you wish to camouflage yourself, to blend in again. Remember that it's a game, and you already know the rules.

Here's some practical advice if you're standing in the same place as me, the paths set so clearly in front of you:

Read. Read a lot. Read books, nonfiction, fan fiction. Read whatever you can put your hands on. I know how hard it is to obtain things in another language when you live outside the USA/Europe. Sign up for free ebooks and newsletters. Read widely and read thoroughly, and absorb all the words you can.

Watch movies and listen to podcasts. Pick up on the dialogue patterns. It's meant for entertainment, but for you, it'll also be a tool. Consume media with a critical eye—look at what they're trying to sell you, look for the strings on the puppets. Google is your friend. Look up images of things you want to write about. Find out what they're called. An image is worth a thousand words.

Write down the words you don't know. Examine them. Learn their origins and roots. Look up expressions and idioms. Get a thesaurus and read through every possible description of hair and skin and fabric texture and furniture shapes, all the silly things they have in English that you never felt the need to know in your language. Learn how to talk about the immortality of the crab or the death of the female calf in their words, and steal them for your own. Craft a thesaurus of descriptions and words that you like, make a list to use as a future resource. When they can't tell the difference between "through," "thorough," "thought," "though," you'll know them even if you're asleep. Find the similarities between your language and English, because all of them have some point of connection. They're all meant for communication.

Practice. Practice in different forms. Write blog posts, essays, poetry, fan fiction. Write a lot, write always. Talk to yourself, out loud. Find out how your voice sounds different in another language, how your narrative flow won't be the same in the two languages you flutter between. It's okay to put a book aside once you finish and start another one. I had to write four whole books in English before I landed my agent.

Find critique partners whose first language is English. Tell them your story and what you want to do. Ask them for help crafting your story. There will be people who doubt you and demean you, but there will also be those who want to help. Those who will know what you're trying to say, and help you say it.

Look around at everything that is being published. People will say that the thing you're writing is doomed to fail, that the market is shrinking, that people simply don't want these kinds of stories anymore. The truth is that for

Writing in Color

as long as humanity has lived and learned how to write and publish stories, we have had an infinite number of mediocre books published. Even a book you hate and think is awful has gotten published. Don't think, *How could anyone ever publish this?* Think, *If this can get published, so can I.*

Even writers whose native language is English make mistakes. Remember this.

You can carve your space. You can make it your own. Your language is not a hindrance. It's not a quirky "accent." You'll always write in your mother tongue, even if the words are coming out in a different language, with different sounds. That is not something negative. It's the mark you'll leave on the world.

You are brave, but not in the way they think.

You are not brave for putting the words on a page, for choosing the distance between yourself and what you are giving to the world. You are not brave for this choice; you simply are what you have always been.

You will face all the challenges head-on, and you will not balk. Lesser people have walked this path before you, people who don't understand their language as well as you do. You will have your language as your torch, as your beacon, and it will obliterate your doubts and your enemies. Your mother tongue is your ally, and when all else fails, it will be there for you. It will conquer and remain unconquered. It will stand boldly, and when people look at you, they might see English, but you are much more.

You will doubt. You will feel you have not done enough.

You will get rejections, and some of them will be because others think you incapable. Some of them will not see your light, but you'll carry on regardless.

You are a vanquisher of idioms. You are a translator of minds.

You are, most of all, a writer, in whichever language you prefer.

Writing in Color

Part Two

JOURNEY
Querying, Publishing, and Beyond

The Publishing Roller Coaster: Navigating the Highs and Lows

BY ADIBA JAIGIRDAR

Adiba Jaigirdar is the award-winning, critically acclaimed, and bestselling author of The Henna Wars, Hani and Ishu's Guide to Fake Dating, *and* A Million to One. *A Bangladeshi/Irish writer and former teacher, she has an MA in postcolonial studies from the University of Kent, England, and a BA in English and history from University College Dublin, Ireland. All of her writing is aided by tea and a healthy dose of Janelle Monáe and Hayley Kiyoko.*

I'll always remember the day I got the offer for my first ever book deal. It was my twenty-fifth birthday, and in my neighboring country my great-aunt was on her deathbed. I already had this call scheduled with an editor, and I was excited. It was my first ever call with an editor! I also felt guilty *because* I was excited.

Still, I had my phone call with birthday cake on my bedside table, bubbling with anxiety and excitement at all the possibility of achieving my dreams. About an hour later there was an offer in my email inbox, and we got a phone call that my great-aunt had passed away.

It was bittersweet, and I remember not really knowing how to feel. Later, my mom said, "We'll always remember the day your great-aunt died because it was your birthday," and I thought, *I'll* always remember it because it was a pivotal step in achieving my lifelong dream.

You don't always have a death in the family alongside an offer of a book deal, but this is just one of the roller coasters that publishing will throw at you. That feeling of overwhelming joy, shadowed by sadness or grief or loss.

Something I also felt over and over during my querying journey.

The Ups and Downs of Querying and Submission

For those unfamiliar with querying, one of the first steps in traditional publishing is searching for a literary agent to represent you and your books. This is referred to as querying. It involves authors emailing potential agents with a query letter consisting of a story pitch, and some sample pages of a completed manuscript.

Querying is *not* easy by any means. It's pinning your dreams on your sleeve and hoping that someone wants to take the risk to make those dreams come true. It's days and months and years of hoping when you're receiving rejection after rejection that make it very, *very* difficult to have any hope at all. It's manuscript after manuscript shelved and collecting dust, wondering if you're good enough to have an agent, to be published, to have all your dreams . . . wondering *when* you'll be good enough for all of those things. Even though I had been writing for a long time, and had many books written before I ever got my first book deal, I didn't start querying until 2017. I was afraid and had told myself that I wasn't good enough. I didn't need anybody else to tell me that too. But something changed in 2017. I wrote something that I *did* think was good enough, though from its swift death in the query trenches, not many agreed.

But querying that first book hardened me, so when I started querying my second book, I went in with the expectation of rejection. Every time I received a rejection, it rolled off me like it was nothing. But surprisingly, querying this time around was a much more pleasant experience. My book was more marketable. It was a queer romance starring people of color at the heels of popular books-turned-movies like *Love, Simon*; *To All the Boys I've Loved Before*; and *Crazy Rich Asians*. It was the right book at the right time. The stars had aligned.

I received a steady stream of full requests from agents, followed by not one, not two, but *three* offers. I could hardly believe it. One of my friends told me that I should really enjoy this moment when agents were trying to win me over to sign with them, because that moment would soon come crashing down. But I didn't expect it to come crashing down so soon. Because even with my offers in hand, I was receiving rejections left and right from all the agents I had nudged with my offer of representation. Some of the rejections were very kind; some of them were downright weird. And again, I felt guilty because even as I was experiencing this epic high of *finally* having offers of representation, of *finally* being out of the query trenches, of *finally* being able to sign with an agent and start my career as an author . . . I was also feeling dejected from all these rejections. I felt like I was being ungrateful because I had what I wanted: an offer. What gave me the right to feel dejected when so many authors dreamed of being where I was? When just days ago, *I* had dreamed of being where I was? After all, it's not like I expected every single agent I queried to make an offer.

But I realize now that the way I felt was probably

because I had been hardened by querying. So, when I was getting rejections before, I had built up my walls. But once I had an offer, I let my walls down. Weirdly, I felt the rejections much more strongly *after* my offers of representation than *before*.

And then things got worse. With my new agent, I revised my book in the space of a few weeks, and then it was off to submissions. My agent and I both had high hopes. It was a high-concept book. It was romance at a time when everyone was looking for romance. It delved into some important topics that were difficult to find in YA at the time (and still are now, to be perfectly honest). But . . . very few people seemed to see the book for all its potential. My editor, the one I had a call with on the day my great-aunt died, made her offer on the book about two months into the submission process. I was ecstatic because I loved my editor. I loved her enthusiasm for my book, and I loved what she had to bring to the table. But none of that changed the fact that it was my *only* offer, it was for a very small amount of money, and the publisher in question was a small press.

Again, my offer of publication came at the heels of a *lot* of rejection. I tried to hold on to the happy feeling of my offer, but it was hard. I felt guilty once more. I realized that I *should* be riding a high because my book, the one that I had poured so much of myself into, was finally going to get published. In some ways, I was riding a high. But I was also sad because I was still getting rejections. Because I was comparing myself to all of the people around me who went on submission one day and had a six-figure offer the next.

To the people with the splashy deals and big publishers. I didn't want to compare, and I didn't want to feel bad. But we can't control our feelings, and unfortunately negative feelings have a way of creeping in even when we're at the top of the world.

This is really what the publishing roller coaster is. Publishing is designed in a way that your highest highs are often accompanied by your lowest lows. It's not something we often talk about either, so that probably makes people feel even worse. When I felt disappointed that no other publisher was willing to take a chance on my story, I felt like I could never speak it aloud to anyone. Because it made me sound ungrateful. When I felt sad that my three offers of representation were followed by a barrage of rejections (including one from someone I then considered my "dream" agent), I kept my mouth shut about it. I didn't want people to think I wasn't happy to have received my offers, because I *was*.

The way publishing works is that you often get a yes, be it from an agent or a publisher. And the singular yes is used to nudge everyone else to also say yes. But usually, it leads to a lot of rejection. So by the structure of publishing, your highs and your lows operate side by side. And it's natural to feel disappointment at your rejections, even if you feel happy about your offer. It's natural to wonder, What if something different had happened?

I've experienced these side-by-side publishing highs and lows throughout my entire career as a writer. As I said, it started with my querying journey . . . and it didn't stop there.

Dreaming and Grieving

In May 2021 my second novel, *Hani and Ishu's Guide to Fake Dating*, released. It's a book that was one of the most joyous things I had written, just by virtue of how much I enjoyed writing it. I'll always remember spending two weeks in my brother and sister-in-law's apartment on holiday, writing thousands upon thousands of words every day to get to the end of the book. It was like no writing experience I had had before. The writing flowed out of me, and I was enjoying every moment of it. By the time I wrote the last line, I didn't care what happened with this book. I cared that I had had such a fun time creating this story and its characters. Still, I expected that my publishing journey with it would follow the trajectory of my joy while writing it.

I couldn't have been more wrong.

Despite how much I loved writing the book, the process of publishing it sent me down a spiral of depression that I had never really experienced before in my publishing career. There were a lot of things at play. For one, I felt unstable in my career itself. Despite my first book having been successful, I was on submission with my fourth novel, and all I was getting were rejections from publishers. It's very difficult to feel confident in your work when you feel like publishers are completely unwilling to take a chance on it.

There was also the fact that I had written the book in 2019, before a worldwide pandemic ravaged the world and changed pretty much everything. I revised the book in lockdown while promoting my debut, unsure of what exactly would happen. Before the pandemic, I had felt somewhat prepared for publishing. But living these past few years with Covid breathing down our necks means that everything about publishing and my career has been unprecedented. It's like trying to build a house from a faulty blueprint—one wrong thing and the entire house can come crashing down.

During this time, one of my uncles passed away from Covid, my dad was diagnosed with cancer, and my grandmother's doctors found a tumor in her brain that they thought might be terminal. She went through months of an experimental treatment in the lead-up to my book's release.

On the twenty-fifth of May my book was released in the US, and on that same day my grandmother passed away. My family and I watched on Zoom as the doctors came to mark the time of death, and we all began to make funeral arrangements that would be viewable via Zoom. My grandmother passed away in the US, where she lived with my uncle, but the other three of her children and all her grandkids live across the world: in Ireland, the United Kingdom, Canada, and the United Arab Emirates.

I had planned a flurry of virtual events for the release of my book and promptly canceled all of them. My virtual launch was set for two hours after my grandmother's time of death, and I remember typing out a tweet through tears that there had been a death in my family and so the event would be canceled. It was supposed to be a celebratory day . . . a day when I would be able to acknowledge all the hard work I had done for this book. But it was marked by death.

Three days later, the day after my book released in the UK, my dad had to go in for a major surgery for his cancer.

So while my family was dealing with my grandmother's passing, we were also worrying about my dad's health and his surgery. Nobody really had time to think about my book release or the launch events I had had to cancel.

Still, in the in-between, my brother drove me around to a few bookshops to sign books. That was when I saw my book in the shops for the first time ever. Due to the pandemic, bookshops being closed, and my books not being published in Ireland and the UK until 2021, I had never had that experience before.

It was surreal—because again this was a major life moment for me. A milestone in my career, the achievement of a lifelong dream, once more marred by grief.

This isn't to say that every author faces setbacks in the form of grief. I think most authors probably don't lose their last grandparent, whom they lived with for most of their childhood, on the day of their book release. But that is the reality of life. Our achievements don't always look the way we want them to look. They're not always sunshine and rainbows, and the intense happiness we want them to be. There are complex feelings that are a result of releasing a book, and they can happen for a variety of reasons.

For me, one of those reasons was the personal things I was dealing with at the time, much of which I felt like I had to bottle up in order to promote my book for months and months.

So, how do you deal with that?

There's no easy answer to that question, as much as I wish there was.

I think the first step to dealing with these really complicated feelings is to try to be as honest with yourself as you possibly can be. Because publishing a book is often seen as a *dream*, as something that's very difficult to achieve, once we cross a milestone to help us achieve that dream, we feel like we lose the right to complain. After all, how can we complain about achieving what we've dreamed of our entire life?

But we can and should be honest about the things that we're feeling. Whether it is pure, unadulterated happiness, or happiness marred by disappointment or grief. The more truthful we are about our feelings, the easier it usually is to deal with them and come out on the other side happier.

It's also really important to have people you love and trust who you feel comfortable sharing your publishing journey with. Not just the high points, but also the low points. It doesn't have to be someone who is in publishing, but it probably helps if they understand the publishing landscape. It should be someone who can be a shoulder for you to cry on, someone who celebrates your achievements and sympathizes with your low points (and obviously someone you can reciprocate this with).

Publishing in the Intersections

One of the reasons publishing can be so difficult is because we are often telling stories that are so important and personal to us. Especially as marginalized individuals, we are often writing the stories that we've never seen before, the stories that we wish had been on shelves when we were younger. So the weight of them feels heavy, not just for us personally, but sometimes even for the world at large.

When we face rejections, many of them can be targeted to our identities. Rejections like *there's already one book representing this particular identity and we don't want to acquire any more* are not exactly rare. I remember a rejection for my debut that said they really wanted a book that was exactly my identity, and exactly the identities of the characters I was writing . . . but they simply didn't want my book. It's difficult not to get beaten down by comments like that.

And as much as I wish I could say it stops once you have an agent, or a book deal, or your book is published, or you become a bestseller . . . it doesn't stop! The first review I ever received was a four-star review that tagged me on social media. It was a nice review, complimenting my writing style and my Bengali characters. Then it ended with a completely homophobic line that totally invalidated my identity and the identity of my characters. I felt like I had been duped by the four stars, the tag, the lovely words and compliments . . . only to be punched in the gut by the horrific homophobia. But this was just the start of it all. As time went by, I realized it wasn't rare to get raving reviews that misidentified me. Worse, raving reviews that were horrendously racist, homophobic, Islamophobic . . . or a wonderful combination of all three! Some of my readers, who are wonderful champions of my books usually, will turn around and say the most horribly racist things sometimes. It's not a rare occurrence, and simply one of those things that happens when you exist at the intersection of marginalizations.

At first, when these things happened, I felt it deep in my soul. I was crushed. I had put so much of myself into my work, and it was horrible to not have that recognized, especially when it came from people in the communities I myself belonged to. Insult my book, my writing, whatever . . . but to be bigoted while complimenting me? To miss the point so much that you love my stories but dehumanize me? It was not a fun experience, and it's still not a fun experience.

The more time went on, the less I cared about these things. The less they affected how I thought of myself, my characters, my stories.

How to Care Less

There are a few important things that helped me separate myself from how I was being affected by these harmful interactions.

First of all, I set up my own sense of success.

There are three types of success you can achieve in publishing:

Sales success: this is where you feel successful when your book is commercially successful. It's selling a lot of copies, maybe you earn out your advance, or earn a lot in royalties.

Social success: this is where you feel successful depending on how people around you are viewing your work. This means that your sense of success is tied into respect from your peers, or even critical recognition. It can be marked by things like starred reviews, librarian and teacher support, reader support, your favorite authors giving you blurbs or talking your book up.

Self success: this is the success that you measure for yourself. It's a boundary you set up for yourself, and only you really know what you need to do to reach this level of success.

For most of us, success is tied up in a combination of all three of these things, but because of how the publishing industry is set up, we're often encouraged to value social and sales success. Our publishers want to make money from the books they've acquired from us, and they want us to achieve critical recognition. It also helps that it's pretty easy to track these kinds of successes. I get a starred review from *Kirkus*? That's success! I sell ten thousand copies? Hit the *New York Times* bestseller list? I'm successful! But the problem is, this sense of accomplishment is often fleeting, and we, along with publishing itself, keep moving the goalposts for ourselves. Making it really, really difficult to hold on to the sense of accomplishment.

You can sell ten thousand copies and feel amazing that so many people have taken a chance on your book. But then you're worrying that it hasn't hit any bestseller list, or won any awards, or received any starred reviews. Or your book *does* achieve all of those milestones, but you have another book coming out in a few months and you're worried it won't measure up to the success of *this* one, which has achieved so much.

So, I have learned to prioritize my self success over everything else. The most important thing I wanted to do as an author was have at least one reader feel connected to my characters and stories. I wanted one reader to feel seen

Writing in Color

in the way I had wanted to be seen when I was a teenager. After all, this was one of my motivations for writing my debut novel, so it just made sense that it was my primary goal.

I achieved it many times over, because a lot of readers have told me about the ways that they've connected to my story and my characters. And it didn't matter so much when I didn't hit these other milestones that we view as leading to the success of a book. I felt successful in what I had set out to do.

Even now, with each book that I publish, I set up my own sense of success before all else. I prioritize it, because it's the only sense of accomplishment that I can really hold on to.

This is simply one of the things you can do to ground yourself in the publishing world.

Another important step is to separate the dream from reality. Throughout this essay, I've spoken about how publishing a book has been one of my lifelong dreams, how getting an agent or a book deal or any achievements in this publishing world feels like a dream. This is the case for a lot of people. Publishing seems unachievable and inaccessible in a lot of ways. And until you're in the business of writing and publishing books, you probably haven't met a *ton* of people who write and publish books. It's a big deal!

But when we keep seeing publishing as a dream, we set ourselves up for really big disappointments. One of the best things I did to ground myself was learn how to see publishing as less than a dream. Despite whatever glitz and glamour may exist in our *heads* about publishing pre–becoming an author, this is not really what publishing or being an author looks like. The sooner we establish for ourselves that publishing is a business and we're doing a job, the easier it is to be able to view everything in publishing realistically and set up real expectations and goals.

You may be thinking that looking at publishing like this seems like having a bit of a pessimistic attitude. But I think the sooner you start viewing things like this, the better you can *actually* dream.

One of the important things that I do at the start of the year is set up my goals for the next year. A major part of this is my publishing goals. So my goals may include things like writing my next young adult rom-com or writing a book in a new genre or age category. Or revising a book or working on my options book, which is the next book my publisher may consider for publication . . . any number of things, really! These are always the things that are in *my* control.

Separately, I dream. My publishing dreams can be things like selling one of the books I'm writing, or hitting a bestseller list, or getting nominated for an award. These are always the things that are *not* in my control.

When I establish these two lists, I'm actively separating my goals (things I can work towards) from my dreams (things that may or may not happen despite however hard I work). I'm taking away the idea that *I* have power over these big publishing things that I actually have nothing to do with. That I can't really influence.

At the end of the day, this makes me feel *really* great

Writing in Color

when I do achieve something that's a "dream," and it doesn't make me feel too disappointed when I don't achieve a "dream" that I had hoped that I would. It doesn't eliminate disappointments, but it helps a little.

Writing down a list isn't immediately going to solve everything, though. It's important for you to really understand the separation that exists between what you can work towards in publishing, and what things are out of your hands. And a lot of things are out of our hands.

But there are things *in* our hands as well.

Finding Control in an Out-of-Control Publishing World

One of the most common pieces of writing/publishing advice you'll probably hear is that writing is the only thing you can control in publishing, so work on that and worry less about the other things. It's definitely a good piece of advice, because at times it *does* feel like writing is the only thing we can control.

But I believe there are other things we can control. One of those is our own personal boundaries, and one of the most important things I've learned and sometimes I'm still learning is how to establish my own boundaries in the publishing industry.

Establishing boundaries can look like a lot of different things. It can mean recognizing that your mental health needs you to not be on social media. Or that you can be on Instagram, but not on Twitter. It can mean that you can be on social media, but you have to limit your time there. Or limit how you interact with readers. It can mean turning off your DMs or curating your replies or making sure nobody can tag you in any pretty Instagram photos, lest one of them be a bigoted rant that sends you down an anxiety spiral.

It can also look like saying no to a blurb request or recognizing which kinds of events you want to do and which ones you'd rather skip. It can mean prioritizing your mental health by cutting back on the amount of time you can give to writing or publishing or promoting a book.

Sometimes it's scary to set up these boundaries because publishing makes us feel like we have to give it our everything. And if we don't, and our books don't do well, we're culpable for it. That's simply not true. We don't have to give our everything to publishing, and that shouldn't be an expectation. Learning to prioritize myself and my mental health was a difficult but gradual thing in my publishing journey. There are still times that I struggle to set boundaries, and there are times when I struggle with the boundaries I've set for myself and wonder if maybe I should do more of this or that.

The important thing is to be able to check in with yourself and change and adjust your boundaries as needed. Nothing is written in stone.

As I'm writing this essay, I'm in my third year of being a published author and looking forward to publishing my third novel at the end of the year. As much as I'd like to say that by my third year I'm at a point where I can deal with everything, and know everything, it's sadly not true.

Publishing throws a lot of curveballs our way. And the more established we become as writers and the longer our

Writing in Color

careers, the more hope and expectations we gather for ourselves. Our first book didn't hit a certain milestone? We want our second book to do that, or our third, or the one after that. Our wants and expectations don't stop, and sadly, neither does the publishing roller coaster.

Still, I'd like to think that in my third year as a published author, I'm a little better at managing the emotional roller coaster. This doesn't mean there aren't days where I feel utterly dejected, or days where I feel joyous, or days where I'm somewhere right in the middle of those feelings.

What I've actually learned from the past few years is to give weight to my feelings, and to process them in healthy ways. I've learned to set realistic expectations, and to find the people who are in my corner to support me, and who I can support in turn. I've learned to set my boundaries, and to prioritize myself and my mental health.

And I've learned that sometimes you can feel really grounded, and really capable of handling anything, and still fall apart. Part of publishing—part of life—is that you're not always ready to deal with everything. There are surprises around every corner. The most you can do is keep going, keep learning, keep trying your best.

That's what I'm doing, and I hope I get to continue doing it for a long time to come. And for any of you reading this anthology who have been struggling, I hope you realize that you're not alone in any of these struggles. We're all going through these different, complex things alongside our publishing journey, and they're not always easy to cope with. I wish I had easy answers and I wish I could tell you how to make the publishing roller coaster feel less like a roller coaster and more like a straightforward motorway. Sadly, that's not how this works.

But I hope that as I've learned from my experiences, you can take something away from them too.

Writing in Color

Breaking All the Rules

BY CINDY PON

Cindy Pon is the author of Silver Phoenix
(Greenwillow), *which was named one of
the Top Ten Fantasy and Science Fiction
Books for Youth by the American Library
Association's* Booklist *and one of 2009's
Best Fantasy, Science Fiction and Horror
by* VOYA; Serpentine *and* Sacrifice
(Month9Books), *which were both Junior
Library Guild Selections and received
starred reviews from* School Library Journal
and Kirkus, *respectively; and* Want *(Simon
Pulse), also a Junior Library Guild Selection,
a near-future thriller set in Taipei.* Ruse,
*the sequel, is out. She is the cofounder of
Diversity in YA with Malinda Lo.*

"Why is this fantasy?" the editor asked. "It's like *Crouching Tiger* crossed with Amy Tan." He did not say it like this was a good thing.

The year was 2008, and I had just finished *Silver Phoenix*, the first novel I had ever written. Having accomplished this incredible (to me) feat, I thought I'd try and get an agent and perhaps sell the novel. Because why not? I attended a big local writers' conference where I could pay a fee to have editors and agents read twelve pages I submitted, meet in person, and receive ten minutes of feedback. It's been many years since 2008, but I still remember feeling so excited, nervous, and hopeful.

"Asian fantasy doesn't sell," he told me matter-of-factly. This editor of a science fiction and fantasy imprint gave me his contact information and made the pretense of keeping my pages after our brief discussion. I'm not sure why he bothered. He told me very clearly what he thought I was trying to publish—something that readers did not want and would not buy.

I was crushed after that conference. As a new writer trying to break into publishing, I had no delusions that it would be easy. But like all writers, I grew up as a voracious reader, and fantasy soon became my favorite as I entered my teen years and young adulthood. It wasn't until I finished *Silver Phoenix* that I realized I had never read a fantasy novel with a character who looked like me. The only times I saw myself in books were in titles like *Farewell to Manzanar* or *The Good Earth*—good books by their own right, but where were the adventures and the battles? When did characters who looked like me get to save the world?

> *We would be very interested to look at a young adult or children's contemporary fiction manuscript that explores Chinese culture and traditions. If you have worked on a piece such as this, please send it to us. And, if you work on one in the future, we'd be very interested to read it.* (Silver Phoenix *agent rejection*)

Despite how crestfallen I felt after that rejection, I'm ridiculously stubborn. I decided I would query as many agents as I could as long as I still felt passionate about getting *Silver Phoenix* out into the world. I would go on to query over one hundred agents, racking up one hundred and twenty-one rejections along the way. During those months, I wandered into a local Barnes & Noble and browsed the children's section for my own kids. There on the top shelf was Lisa Yee's middle-grade novel *Millicent Min, Girl Genius* staring back at me. I vividly recall picking up the book in wonder, as I'd never seen an Asian girl on a children's book cover before. Years later, Lisa (who is a delight) and I would become friends, but in that moment, I was very much alone in my querying journey, and seeing this book heartened me. It told me it was indeed possible for *Silver Phoenix* to be published too. I'd just have to keep trying.

> *Your writing is really lovely, and I see*
> *some great potential there. However, I just*
> *couldn't see this fitting into the current YA*
> *market, and I don't think it would work*
> *for the adult trade market either.* (Silver
> Phoenix *agent rejection*)

I was quickly running out of agents to query, and I considered submitting to small presses on my own (many of which did not require agented queries at the time) if all else failed. But luckily, I was able to sign with Bill Contardi at Brandt & Hochman some months later. We went immediately out on submission after some light edits. (As an aside, I prefer a noneditorial agent because I know how people envision the best story to be personal and different. I have also known too many writing friends who did extensive and repeated edits for their agent, which led nowhere. Of course, I have successful author friends who have agents who edit well. Still I firmly believe major edits lie with the editor who acquires your book, not your agent.)

Astoundingly, *Silver Phoenix* went to auction. I didn't even know that "auction" was the correct term for it when I spoke with the three editors who were offering on my debut. I was incredulous and elated, and *Silver Phoenix* along with its sequel, *Fury of the Phoenix*, were acquired by Greenwillow Books. My editor told me that she was unable to come up with any comps (comparable titles) for the acquisitions team—something that is pretty vital when you try to buy a novel. The only books she could think of were Tales of the Otori written by Lian Hearn, which were adult titles. This was another hurdle I didn't realize my books would deal with—with no precedent or a similar title and its sales history, my books were an unknown risk. Sure, many young adult fantasies had been published before, but never an Asian-inspired one. It would be some years later that I realized *Silver Phoenix* was the very first young adult Asian fantasy published by a major publisher here in the United States.

Despite that distinction, my debut fell into a black hole. *Silver Phoenix* was released with a gorgeous cover prominently featuring a Chinese girl and basically tanked. I debuted in 2009 right amidst a terrible recession. Borders skipped carrying the title, and Barnes & Noble stocked it limitedly. Readers who were excited for my book could not find it. My debut was groundbreaking, yet no one knew about it. In my view, it never got the marketing or publicity for being special—instead my book was considered niche and an outlier, not for mass-market consumption.

The sequel to *Silver Phoenix*, *Fury of the Phoenix*,

released two years later in 2011 after a very controversial cover change that was distressful and disheartening for me as the author. I understood the ire against the new *Silver Phoenix* cover and repackaging, which featured a headless heroine with obscured ethnicity, with a sequel cover to match, but where were these people to support the original cover displaying the Chinese heroine when it was released?

Around that same time, some authors were coordinating big group signings and tours. These events were mainly composed of lead title authors, and at the time, that meant nearly all white authors. Marginalized writers simply were not striking the lead title deals in young adult at the time. I had joked with Malinda Lo that we should organize our own tour—a tour that was the opposite of these all-white author tours. And when her Asian young adult fantasy *Huntress* and my sequel *Fury of the Phoenix* were set to release within a month of each other (the only two young adult Asian fantasies released that year by a major publisher), I somehow got Malinda to agree on coordinating our own tour.

The Diversity in YA tour launched in San Francisco joined by Gene Yang, whom I had tracked down at San Diego Comic-Con International and asked to participate. "You have to say yes," I pleaded, and Gene said yes. We had never met before that day. Our next stop was in Austin, then Chicago, Cambridge, and New York. We wrapped up the tour in October in San Diego. Malinda and I did all of the organizing and publicity, and paid for the cost of the tour ourselves. Because we could not pay for authors to attend, we had to choose cities where authors who could participate were located. Besides Gene Yang, Nnedi Okorafor joined us in Chicago, and Jacqueline Woodson in New York, among many other fantastic writers. It truly is wonderful to see the trajectory these authors' careers have taken since 2011, including for Malinda Lo herself—I could not have asked for a better friend or partner in this endeavor. It was a stressful whirlwind for us, but I only have very fond memories of that tour.

There was something very empowering in doing this ourselves, because it would never have been done otherwise. The conversation in regard to diversity and inclusiveness in children's and young adult books was almost nonexistent at the time, and any dialogue that might have emerged was short-lived and forgotten. The tour garnered some attention among readers and within the industry, followed by a write-up in the *Atlantic*, but the dialogue did not really reach its necessary peak and momentum until We Need Diverse Books emerged on the scene in 2014, three years later. I would like to think that Diversity in YA helped to seed this important dialogue in some way.

Traditional publishing is old and entrenched in its thinking and processes. My experiences in searching for and boosting nondominant narratives for the Diversity in YA website truly showed how long it takes publishing to pivot. "Pivot" isn't even the right word for this behemoth, and as I write this piece more than a decade later, there is still much work to be done. We've seen in recent years in surveys how predominantly white publishing is—and this extends from publicity to marketing, booksellers, and librarians. This is what we mean when we say the problem is systemic. When it comes to stories, so many editors aim to see their own narratives in what they acquire. Whatever the exciting difference or edginess is, it can't be that different. It can't push them outside of their comfort zones. And this is exactly what we, as marginalized writers, often bring to the table—stories that might not seem familiar enough, stories that challenge the status quo, stories that don't feel as "relatable."

Unfortunately, my sales for the debut did not "meet expectations," making it almost impossible for me to sell another Asian young adult fantasy. BookScan numbers followed me like a stalker spewing half-truths. Because I was stubborn, I was determined to bring more into the world for readers. More for teen Cindy, who never got to see herself in these kinds of stories she loved.

I decided to write *Serpentine*, uncontracted, which was a story focused on a handmaid–turned–serpent demon featuring a strong sister friendship. Shape-shifters were always popular, and in 2011 there was no panicked chatter of young adult fantasy being an overcrowded and bloated market. I poured my heart and soul into this book, and Bill sent *Serpentine* out on submission in 2013.

It didn't take long for the rejections for *Serpentine* to roll in.

> *Cindy is an imaginative writer but I think*
> *this would be a tough sell . . . judging by*
> *the way a few recent books that were also*

well written and played with a similar kind
of mythos fared (positive critical response
but poor sales). But she is talented and I
would be interested in seeing other projects
of hers in the future. (Serpentine editor
rejection)

This editor was referring specifically to an African-inspired fantasy novel written by an author from that background. Not only was Asian fantasy seen as niche and the reason a book might not have commercial success, but my title was compared with another non-white fantasy title—both seen as not meeting sales "expectations." Was that editor I met at the conference right in the end? Asian fantasy doesn't sell?

I had so many editors who were "fans" of mine. But no one who would actually acquire *Serpentine*.

Thanks so much for sending this project my
way. I love Cindy's storytelling and the way
she so beautifully elevates the fantasy. In
some ways, this reminded me of the legends
of Melusine.

But I worry that the transformation into
a half-serpent with a forked tongue is going
to be a tough sell to the YA readership. And
given that her sales history already presents
a bit of a challenge, I'm afraid I'll have to
pass. (Serpentine editor rejection)

Writing in Color

A couple editors asked if I could write something, anything, other than Asian fantasy. Remember, even in 2012 and 2013, when Bill diligently submitted my manuscript, there was still less than a handful of Asian young adult fantasies published by the major publishers—none of which did well. (And if you looked deeper, none of which got support from their publishers or the big marketing push that lead titles received. That wouldn't happen for an Asian American debut author writing young adult fantasy until 2017.)

> *Cindy is a wonderful writer, and I'd love to*
> *see something else from her. But something*
> *that's a big departure—contemporary?*
> *Realistic?—would be more compelling,*
> *given her sales track. (*Serpentine *editor*
> *rejection)*

I quickly learned that as a marginalized writer trying to tell a story from my lens, you only got one chance to make yourself a success—if you ever got that chance at all. So many types of novels can fail to meet expectations, and get a second or even third chance. But when it came to fantasies drawing from non-Western mythos, publishing was not so generous or forgiving. It reminded me of Margaret Cho's Asian American sitcom *All-American Girl*, which premiered in 1994 and tanked badly. It would be over two decades later until Hollywood took another chance with an Asian American sitcom—*Fresh Off the Boat* aired in 2015. Asian narratives were considered too niche, too foreign, and not relatable. They were too risky and they wouldn't sell. This is a self-fulfilling prophecy that marginalized creators are plagued with by white gatekeepers who decide what types of books are published and what kinds of shows and movies make it to the screen.

Sometime during all of this, I met with my agent, Bill Contardi, over lunch and reiterated my desire to get more young adult Asian fantasy out into the world. I remember him telling me that I needed to understand the market, that I should look to see what kinds of young adult novels were selling. I also recall very clearly my response to him: I *do* know the young adult market—I don't want to write white angels. It was my *you're either with me or you can leave me* conversation. Much to my surprise, Bill stuck it out with me, and he was my agent for over a decade until he retired.

After nearly two years on submission, *Serpentine* and its sequel, *Sacrifice*, were acquired by Month9Books, a small press. The books sold for six hundred dollars each, a considerable drop from when *Silver Phoenix* went to auction a few years back. I was paid a respectable midlist price for those titles by Greenwillow, and it would also be the biggest advance I would see in my career as an author. I remember divulging my advance for *Serpentine* to a fellow author, who literally sputtered and said, *You'd get more if you self-published*. Which was probably true. But I had done my homework, and I knew that for young adult titles, it was really challenging to get them into libraries if they did not receive trade reviews from the likes of *School Library Journal*, *Publishers Weekly*, *Booklist*, et cetera. I grew up loving libraries, and it was important to me that my books were available to kids through libraries. As an author, you will definitely be presented with rough journeys and tough choices. Only you can truly answer what matters to you as an author and which path you'll take. No two people will ever have the same experience. This is so in publishing as it is in life.

The next few years was me hustling. *Serpentine* received glowing reviews from the industry and was a Junior Library Guild Selection but was not carried in Barnes & Noble. Being stocked in brick-and-mortar stores is still crucial for children's and young adult titles, and if you're skipped, it's a challenging path for the novel as far as sales. I pitched myself to book festivals, attended conferences for BookExpo America (now defunct) and the American Library Association, all of which I paid for out of pocket. I spent a lot of money to attend these events and get *Serpentine* in front of readers, teachers, librarians, and booksellers. I consider this duology to be my best work to date, and it is the least known and read.

Writing is so strange as it can be so isolating. That's how it was for me at least, in the beginning, as a new author. I wrote on hope, belief, and perhaps misplaced ambition. It really wasn't until *Serpentine* released, and I was hustling trying to promote it and attending those festivals and conventions, that I realized how many people were there to help. They got me an invitation when all the other authors were pitched by a big-publisher publicist, offered a hotel room for me to crash at when my personal budget was stretched, offered to blurb my books, talked them up on Twitter, or ordered them into their indie bookstores. This business is hard, and it often is harder for those of us writing nondominant narratives, but I'm truly grateful for all the people who helped to lift me along the way, from all backgrounds. I would never have gotten so far in my publication journey without them.

I consider fantasy my first love, and it is the genre I most enjoy writing. But stubborn as I am, even I had to admit traditional publishing did not want more Asian fantasy novels from me. But several editors were open to seeing something entirely different—something new. I went back to the short story I wrote for the *Diverse Energies* anthology (Tu Books) and decided to try to expand it into a novel. It was my first non-fantasy published and intrigued me enough that I felt I could make it work. That was how *Want* was born.

I've never felt imposter syndrome before, but the closest I've come is to be called a science-fiction writer. *Want* was an outlier and pushed me so much out of my comfort zone, I dropped my daily word count from one thousand words a day to five hundred. As a writer, I'm super easy on myself and celebrate every small forward motion, even if it is one hundred words. Even if it is fifty! If you aren't your own greatest cheerleader, who will be?

But the *doubt* I felt when I started writing this book. I took a research trip to Taipei in 2013, and much of what I heard, saw, and experienced there made it into the novel. *Want* truly was an ode to my birth city, and that was a strong incentive for me to *try*. Still, this novel challenged me in multiple ways. As a writer, I'm always looking to level up with each new project, but there's a fine line in trying something new and different versus tackling something that is impossible for your ability yet as a writer.

I was attempting to write from a modern teen boy point of view for the first time in the first person. The language and prose were also different from what I was accustomed to in my fantasy novels. My setting was near-future based on a real city, and I needed to create an ensemble cast for this heist novel—never mind the technology! *Want* took years to write, due to deadlines for other contracted books, and my not being familiar with the genre itself. Holly Black was very helpful in her advice (as always) and suggested I read other cyberpunk novels to get a feel of what the genre was like.

I tried.

I read books by William Gibson and Neal Stephenson, both lauded and well known in the science fiction and fantasy community. I managed to finish one novel between them, then started a couple more and stopped midway. I found the reads very discouraging, because I recognized immediately that this was *not* what I wanted to do with *Want*. Other than the usual dressings with cityscapes wreathed in neon lights and flying vehicles, their narratives and lenses were so different from my own. I remember feeling almost defeated when I was reading these classics.

How does one reconcile the dissonance between your own story and everything that came before it—applauded and held up as the gold standard? As marginalized creators, you can't. You have to make your own rules and set your own standards. I began writing short stories at fourteen years old and didn't even write an Asian character until I was in my twenties. I've read juvenilia (work written as a teen) at book festivals—always a fun and hilarious time. But what I didn't get to say after I left the stage and the laughter died down was how everyone was white in my stories. They had names that I thought white people would have, like Amber and Colleen. They ate meat loaf and potatoes for dinner as they bantered around their formal dining table. Nothing I had ever experienced myself, but things that were spoon-fed to me through books and all other media.

Stories centered around white people.

I remember a San Diego Comic-Con International panel I did with my talented writer and artist friend Nilah Magruder, and she talked about how uncomfortable she used to be drawing brown people. We agreed on how difficult it was for us as marginalized creators, growing up with stories only about white people—how pervasive and insidious that was. I jokingly say now that I write All Asian All the Time, but it certainly was not how I started.

Despite it all, I finished *Want* and went on submission in the fall of 2015. Michael Strother, who was at Simon Pulse at the time, quickly read and replied requesting an R&R (revise and resubmit). But he only wanted me to resubmit a synopsis taking into consideration his editorial notes versus rewriting my entire submission. This obviously would save me a lot of work and time, but also spoke to how he trusted me as a writer. *Want* was acquired by Michael at a time

Writing in Color

when YA science fiction supposedly was not popular. I had been using #cuteasianboys as a tag forever on Twitter, and upon seeing it, Michael had replied, Maybe *Want* needs a cute Asian boy on its cover? He sent me the art by the amazingly talented Jason Chan right before Michael left Simon Pulse. I went on to work with Jennifer Ung on *Want* and *Ruse* and felt very fortunate to do so. But Michael has since left publishing entirely, and it truly is a tremendous loss for writers and readers alike.

As difficult as it is for marginalized writers to sell their books in traditional publishing, I know that it is just as challenging for non-white editors to get our books acquired, having to pitch them to acquisitions teams that often only rely on past successes and numbers as a guide to what can be successful in the future. Again, think about the first editor who told me that Asian fantasy doesn't sell—how that cycle perpetuates itself.

Want would go on to be my fifth published title and the best known. It was carried widely in Barnes & Noble and supported generously by independent bookstores. Its momentum and wider readership I attribute entirely to word of mouth, and I could not be more grateful for those wonderful readers who spread the love via social media and blog posts.

I wanted to conclude this piece by noting two incidents that stood out to me in my decade-plus author career, and both took place in 2016, while I was promoting *Serpentine*. The first was when an Asian American reader asked me at a con if I felt tremendous pressure as one of the few Asian

American writers publishing Asian fantasy. He asked if I worried I would do it wrong, and if it stopped me from creating. My answer was an immediate no, and his face very clearly registered surprise. I suspected that he, too, was a writer, and I wanted to convey that we should not self-reject when it comes to our stories.

As an immigrant from Taiwan and with an ESL (English as a Second Language) background, I understand what it is like to feel as if you're not *enough*. Not Asian enough for where I came from and certainly not "American" enough for where I am. It is a duality that many of us are familiar with, and our stories matter more than we can know. More than ever in this day and age. No story is perfect and likely someone will feel you have done it wrong. But as long as you approach your writing with respect and thought and research, don't self-reject out of fear or insecurity. There will be enough roadblocks along the way as it is.

The other incident was when I attended the Romantic Times con in Las Vegas that same year. Two young Korean American women came to introduce themselves to me. They were big fans, they told me, and I could see their shining, beautiful faces in the audience in my panels. I said earlier that writing can feel so isolating. And as someone who wrote the first Asian young adult fantasy only to be told it failed to "meet expectations" and to not write any more Asian fantasy, to meet Asian American readers who found *Silver Phoenix* as teens and enjoyed my debut meant so much to me.

Those readers were also writers: Axie Oh and Kat Cho.

It is a joy to see these young women take publication by storm, spearheading and tackling projects while also creating their own stories and nabbing those book deals. I can't tell you how much this fills my heart, to feel the next wave of writers rising behind me and propelling all of us forward with their drive and ferocity. It is amazing and inspiring. We continue breaking barriers and forging our own paths together. Our voices matter.

So does yours.

Totally Not the Fairest Author of Them All

BY GAIL D. VILLANUEVA

Gail D. Villanueva is a Filipino writer, illustrator, and web designer based in Rizal, Philippines. She is the author of Sugar and Spite (Scholastic) and the Lulu Sinagtala and the Tagalog Gods series (HarperCollins). Her debut novel, My Fate According to the Butterfly (Scholastic), was named a Best Book of the Year by Kirkus Reviews, an Amazon Best Book of the Month Editor's Pick, and an NCSS-CBC Notable Social Studies Trade Book for Young People.

We see this happen in white-authored fairy tales all the time. When villains ask who's the fairest of them all, magic mirrors show princesses and handmaidens who have skin as white as snow. Someone who, without a doubt, isn't dark-skinned like me.

To be fair (pun intended), "fairest" in these old tales could have meant "the most beautiful." It's kind of like saying "fair weather," which describes the weather as pleasant or good. It's also weird, even for a wicked queen with an insecurity as huge as planet Jupiter, to ask her magic mirror who has the whitest skin of all. Right?

Well, not really. Having light skin and being beautiful are easily conflated, especially in my reality, where whiteness is a measure of worth and beauty.

I've made it a lifetime goal to ensure my books break the notion that only those with fair complexions can be in the spotlight. This is evident in the stories I write. But it may surprise you that this aspiration—most often expected of non-white authors to have—was something that I didn't originally want. Learning to love my dark skin was a long, arduous journey of unpacking hurts and societal ills, marred by a very difficult obstacle you'd least expect: me.

I was the villain in my own story.

Growing Up with Skin Not as White as Snow

I spent most of my life before now hating the fact that I had such a dark complexion. It took me a while to unlearn this and to try to make sense of why I felt that way. Because colorism is a complex and destructive construct that plagues not just my community, but many cultures everywhere in the world.

Alice Walker, in an essay published in her 1983 non-fiction collection, *In Search of Our Mothers' Gardens*, defined colorism as "prejudicial or preferential treatment of same-race people based solely on their color." From my understanding, this means colorism is rooted in racism, but with a specific distinction. It's not just about a person oppressing someone of another race—it's about someone oppressing a person who has a darker skin color, *and* they're of the same race.

It's important to note that a lot of Filipinos have dark skin. Don't quote me on that but moving up and down the social-class ladder showed me we aren't a minority. Yet, we still hold whiteness as the main qualifier for privilege and this messed-up standard of beauty.

Don't get me wrong. I love my country and our people. The Philippines is a beautiful melting pot of different cultures, brought on by its archipelagic geography and rich history of trade and colonization. It's this history, perhaps, that came with the cost of colorism to our country.

For 333 years, Spain established in the Philippines a colonial caste system where race determined the privileges (or lack thereof) a person had. Fair-skinned landowners paid less taxes and "pure-blooded" white Spaniards paid none, while my dark-skinned ancestors were taxed the most even when they did most of the work and got paid so little.

The oppressive caste system was abolished when the United States bought the Philippines from Spain for twenty million dollars through the 1898 Treaty of Paris. However, our new American colonizers, with their own racist history, perpetuated the preference for fair complexion during their forty-eight-year reign. The Japanese invasion of the Philippines during World War II made it worse—the atrocities they committed plunged our people deeper into the chasm of self-hate and self-devaluation.

My country is now a democratic republic in these modern times. We're technically no longer under any other country's rule, but we have yet to heal from our colonized past. Whiteness had even become some sort of a status symbol. It romanticized the memories of wealthy, fair-skinned hacienderos gallivanting on their mansions' shaded balconies, while their servants worked these landowners' farms all day under the sweltering rays of the sun.

Colorism is still very much alive in our society, and it's easy to see traces of it *everywhere*. Our groceries have entire lanes of skin whiteners in different forms—soap, moisturizer, lotion, oil, face peel, or whatever beauty product companies can slap the "skin whitener" label on. Advertisements, in print, broadcast, or online, all feature fair-skinned models. Actors with pale complexions are most often (if not always) the stars of a Filipino movie or TV series. Dark-skinned actors are either villains, sidekicks, or comic relief.

The message is loud and clear: white is beautiful, brown is not. As an adult, it constantly tests my self-esteem. I'm able to handle it better now, thankfully. As a kid, though? Well, I was too young to understand the relationship of whiteness, colonization, and classism. But I felt it. I felt every painful bit of it.

I knew I would never be the prettiest in class. How could I, when everyone who was considered "beautiful" had skin that was either fair, fairer, or fairest?

My family also wasn't rich, putting me in the lowest echelons of the classroom—the darker your skin, the poorer you *must* be. My lola helped my parents from time to time so my sister and I could study at an exclusive private school, where my dad was the official photographer. No one ever said to my face that I was ugly because I'm dark (they were probably afraid I'd sabotage their photos in the yearbook or something), but I had classmates who didn't hesitate to tell me that I was "just" the daughter of the school's hired staff. I wasn't rich nor was I beautiful; I wasn't like them at all.

I couldn't do anything to change my skin color, but that doesn't mean I didn't try. I asked my mom to buy me skin-whitener soap, which she gladly did since she wanted to use it too. But she also bought me books, contemporary

Writing in Color

stories about the lives of American kids of Sweet Valley Middle School, Riverdale High, and the Baby-Sitters Club. They were so unlike the traditional fairy tales, Bible stories, and illustrated encyclopedias I read and reread from my grandmother's mini library. I devoured all of them.

Even when I had a crappy day in school, I was comforted by the thought of coming home and escaping to the spooky world of R. L. Stine and Christopher Pike, or going on an investigative adventure with Nancy Drew and the Hardy Boys. Stories became my sanctuary.

Still, it never escaped my notice that none of the characters in these books I loved looked like me.

I figured authors in the West just didn't write about kids who are Filipino, dark, and flat-nosed. Insisting otherwise was like trying to take out the sword in the stone as an unnamed extra and failing, an insignificant character who was simply added to the story so the chosen white boy's triumph looks special. I felt like I was destined to live with this thought, that dark-skinned people such as myself will always just be supporting characters—we can never be the hero. It was the way things were, and I simply accepted it.

If I could downplay the pain, maybe it wouldn't hurt so bad.

But I guess fate had other ideas, leading me to chance upon a conversation between my grandmother and a distant relative by accident.

"Of all your children, your daughter had to be the one who takes after her dark father," the distant relative said to my lola. "Had she been more attractive, she could have married someone better than that poor photographer. Her own children inherited her ugly flat nose and dark skin!"

My grandmother was furious, of course. That relative was never invited to our house ever again. I think the only time I've seen them once more was at my lola's funeral, contrite and full of regret.

But the damage was done.

I hated being brown.

A Publishing Dream Was a Wish My Weary Kiddo Heart Made

My husband often jokes, if you want to get me to do something and do it well, tell me anything that implies I can't do it. He's totally right—I really don't like being undermined and underestimated.

While that distant relative hurt me more than I would ever admit, it gave me something to strive for. I wanted to prove that they were mistaken, that my mom made the right choice—no, the *best* choice—marrying my dad and having me. Sure, maybe I'd never be a fair-skinned beauty queen, but I was talented and smart.

I practiced basketball day in, day out; I became the starting point guard of our school's official team. I honed the techniques my parents taught me at our weekly art workshops; I won art contests in school and in our district. I read a lot, finishing every book I laid my hands on; I found my vocabulary expanding faster than most kids' in my class.

Eventually, my spite-fueled drive to prove that distant

relative wrong became the trappings of a dream I never thought I'd have: to one day become a published writer.

It was a dream I intended to accomplish in the long term. I knew it wasn't happening anytime soon. But as usual, I practiced. I honed my craft. I wrote short stories and made comics. I read every book my mom bought me from cover to cover.

The stories I made had white protagonists, of course. Because that was how things were—brown girls couldn't be heroes, only sidekicks.

I remember going through my grandmother's library after finishing all my book allocation for the month. Like I said, my lola wasn't into fiction much, so imagine my surprise when I found a novel with back cover copy that interested me, *To Kill a Mockingbird* by Harper Lee.

Nope. I didn't become a woke eleven-year-old after reading that book. But it did have me asking this question to my young writer self: Why did it have to be the white girl who told the story of a Black man? Everything revolved around the Black man so much. Couldn't he, or his Black daughter, tell his own story?

Eleven-year-old me then promised herself: one day, I'm going to write an important book like this, but the main character will be Filipino. *Because I'm Filipino.*

Since that day, I went to the bookstore and imagined myself touching a book with my name on it. My book that was as Filipino as a book can be.

Many years passed. I grew up. I took on a business course in college and struggled through all the math parts.

Writing for a living was a wonderful dream to have, but it wouldn't feed my family. I needed to make money.

Still, I never forgot about my publishing dream.

We were having dinner one day when my mom casually asked me if I still wrote short stories. I answered no, but I read a lot and posted my thoughts on my website during my free time. "That's a shame," she said. "Your homeroom teacher told me you're a great writer. I wouldn't have spent so much buying you all those books had I known you'd only abandon the writing thing."

And just like that, my mom lit the fire in me again. I was going to be published, no matter what.

But like any white-authored chosen-one story, I had a lot of false starts.

You see, traditional publishing in the Philippines is very different from the US. Books aren't as accessible—they're mostly imported, and expensive. The very few libraries we have rarely carry fiction titles, mostly just academic texts that students only bother with when they have a book report to submit. There's been *some* improvement in the way things are run, but it's still a very young industry.

So, it's no surprise that self-publishing is thriving here in my country. It gives anyone a chance to see their author name in print, when traditional routes are very prohibitive for nobodies like me.

I gave self-publishing a shot.

It seemed like the most logical thing for me. After all, I had all the tools to make it work. I had at least twenty years of experience in graphic design—I could create and

Writing in Color

give my book a kick-butt book cover. My husband and I run our own design studio, giving me decades-long experience and an established network in advertising. Heck, I could even design and code my own online bookstore if I wanted to.

But it wasn't for me.

I did everything I could to learn more about writing and publishing. I read a lot, and joined as many writing seminars and workshops as I could afford. I responded to every submission open call where my work could meet the barest minimum requirements. Of course, I only got rejections. But I didn't let them deter me. They were learning experiences, after all.

Then, I began to notice some things. There were places that didn't seem to be welcoming to dark brown authors like me. I figured maybe I was just being too sensitive. Competition *was* high. So I still stuck with the writing programs and short story submissions. Wouldn't hurt, right?

Well, yeah, it was fine. That was, until I got told that my main protagonist should always be white, while secondary characters or love interests can be people of color.

I couldn't put my finger on why hearing this made me feel iffy. The only thing I was sure of was that this particular path in publishing wasn't for me.

I started to have doubts if publishing a book with a Filipino main character was even remotely attainable. It felt like a wish that only a fairy godmother could grant and make come true. In short, it was an absolutely, 100 percent impossible dream.

An Ugly Duckling in Predominantly White Publishing

I wanted to publish my book for the world to read, but I felt like an ugly duckling in a yard full of swans.

The seeming impossibleness of my dream didn't deter me, though. The more life threw wrenches on my path, the more determined I became to accomplish my goal of becoming a published author with a very Filipino book.

So, I did my research. I signed up for a Twitter account, which seemed to be the preferred social media platform of writers in the West. I joined forums and writing websites. I taught myself to write a decent query letter and learned to pitch my book and myself to literary agents I'd love to represent me without sounding desperate or trying too hard.

I eventually met fellow authors who wanted to traditionally publish in the US too. As a social butterfly, it was easy for me to befriend anyone, even those whom I probably shouldn't have. So, to keep things clear and on topic but still maintain anonymity, let's refer to them collectively as the "Write Friends."

The Write Friends and I read each other's works and regularly met online or in person, chatting all day about literary agents and publishing info we got from our individual research. Then I got their notes on my book. The Write Friends said I "was not a bad writer," and was "a relatively okay storyteller," but I might want to consider changing my brown Filipino protagonist to a white girl instead. Agents wouldn't be able to relate to my brown lens, lowering my chances of getting offered representation to next to none.

The Write Friends' feedback brought me back to certain writing programs I attended and a few unforgettable rejection letters I received on the short stories I submitted. Didn't they say the exact same thing? *Brown people couldn't be protagonists.*

So, I settled on a compromise: make my main character half white. I wasn't half white, and I definitely wasn't white. I had no idea about the complexities of being biracial. I never experienced (and never will experience) being in proximity of whiteness.

But I was willing to do the work, if that was what it took to get an offer of representation. I figured, once I signed with an agent and published my debut, I'd be able to sell my very Filipino book next. I just needed a foot in the door.

There was a huge red flag waving itself in front of my face. Still, I chose to ignore it. The Write Friends knew better. They were rich, educated, and had skin as fair as those of models on TV and billboard ads. Surely, they were better than me. That said, I would never fit in the ideals of the literary elite. They were like the modern versions of the Illustrados—the moneyed, educated Filipinos of the Spanish colonial period in the late nineteenth century.

The Write Friends soon advanced into their careers. Signing with a publisher, getting an agent, winning awards. Me? I continued to languish in the querying trenches. That was fine, I thought. They were better than me after all.

Maybe the reason I wasn't getting any agent bites was because "not a bad writer" and a "relatively okay storyteller" just weren't good enough. I needed to be better.

With the Write Friends preoccupied, I got to know more people in the writing community. I joined mentoring programs. I had my book read and reviewed by other querying authors I met online. They loved it even though I had such an uncomfortable time writing the half-white protagonist.

As I edited my story, I did more research for it. My book was a historical fantasy set during the 1896 Philippine Revolution. I read more about the spark that lit the Filipinos' desire for freedom from their Spanish colonizers, and how they gave their lives so their descendants could enjoy a democratic republic. I learned about the torture and the pain they went through, the discrimination they experienced.

Now, that's not to say they didn't teach us this in school. They did. But what we got was more of a sanitized, academic version. To be fair, I didn't have the wealth of information on the internet back then. So, it was understandable that my recent, more in-depth research gave me a better glimpse of the atrocities my people experienced under the oppression of our colonizers.

The reason why writing a half-white protagonist in that book felt off to me became clear. I couldn't write it with my whole heart because I didn't have the privilege of whiteness. I'm brown, and a brown person like me would have had a very different experience in such a turbulent time in Philippine history. This book, this half-white book, was not me.

In that time away from the Write Friends, I met another Filipino author online with the similar goal of publishing traditionally in the US. Isabelle and I became friends. She lived on the other side of Metro Manila from me, but we made it work.

I always teased Isabelle for being my "rich friend," but she took it all in stride. Perhaps being a brown Filipino girl from a self-made family and having studied at an international school with white people gave her a more nuanced perspective on racial issues that I couldn't seem to find in the Write Friends. I found myself sharing with Isabelle more life and publishing updates than with the Write Friends, since everything I shared with her was always greeted with enthusiasm and all-out support. Isabelle didn't think I was just a not-bad writer or a "relatively okay storyteller." She believed I was *great*.

For some reason, the Write Friends didn't like seeing me expand my little network. I shrugged it off, though, thinking that maybe they were just stressed out over their own writing and publishing things.

However, even with my definitely not-stellar literary credentials, I remained the Write Friends' go-to person for story-level critique. I was flattered they still trusted me with their beautiful words. Well, they were beautiful words . . . until they used a dehumanizing metaphor for a dark brown girl, made their protagonist cruelly mock the circumstances of another character's immigration, and included a supposedly funny scene where a Filipino character is teased about having dark skin.

Maybe it was because I found a supportive writer friend in Isabelle, or perhaps my research in historical inequalities was changing my perspective in more ways than I thought. Either way, I finally got a face slap from the red flag that had been waving itself in front of me. The jealousy, the passive-aggressive comments, the non-compliments . . . They all finally made sense. To the Write Friends, I wasn't really a "friend" friend, since friendships are built on mutual respect. I was nowhere near being their friend. They didn't even think of me as an equal.

I was beneath them.

Now, you might ask why I should be bothered, when I thought of them as being better than me anyway. My mom always said that I should remember that there's someone out there better than me in things I know I'm good at. It's a humbling thought and has encouraged me to continuously learn and strive to be better.

But it's an entirely different thing when someone thinks of you as less than human. They're fine to be with when they're ahead, but once you start catching up, it's a totally different story.

Being friends with Isabelle taught me what a true author-friendship was like. She made me realize that it was possible for a fellow writer to be supportive even when they're frustrated with their own thing. Everyone's publishing journey is different, so energies are better spent on things we can control—our writing.

Even though I let go of the toxic relationships with the Write Friends (whom we'll now call the "Not Write Friends"), my publishing journey still wasn't all sunshine and rainbows.

My forays without the Not Write Friends in the US writing community were generally welcoming. Writers who are Black, Indigenous, and people of color (BIPOC) help each other. But within those ranks, I still saw cracks brought on by colorism and homogeneity . . . like that time when I was told that I should just publish in my own country.

I get it, though. Really. The system is, and always has been, rigged against anyone who isn't white. Oftentimes, it feels like we're carps in a dirty, too-small pond fighting for those teeny bits of bread thrown at us, while our white contemporaries are enjoying an abundance of expensive fish food in their spacious, beautifully landscaped aquariums. It becomes a dog-eat-dog world for us non-white authors.

Thing is, acknowledging the privilege of white proximity can theoretically imply a non-white person might be prejudiced. And that simply cannot work with the narrative of BIPOC in publishing being woke and unable to be racist—or, for lack of a better term, "colorist."

It doesn't sound as terrible as being considered less than human, but it is as damaging. It brings about a toxic kind of competition within a community that should be helping each other dismantle oppressive ideals in a predominantly white publishing industry.

Isabelle and I eventually found a group of other like-minded author friends while querying. We've held each other's hands since then. I shelved that book with the half-white protagonist and wrote a contemporary story with a bit of magic. This book wasn't the groundbreaking, Harper Lee–esque story my eleven-year-old self imagined writing.

But it was close to my heart. It had a very Filipino cast (and only one white side character) and was inspired by my relationship with my sister. Within its pages were as many of the things I loved and hated about being Filipino as I could put in a middle-grade book.

I had great hopes for this story, and so did the mentors and beta readers who helped me make it better. Once I felt ready, I pitched this new book to agents on my sister's birthday, and I prayed doing so would bring me good luck. And it did. A month into querying this new book, I signed with my agent, Alyssa Eisner Henkin.

Alyssa's enthusiasm for my work renewed my weary kiddo heart's wish of publishing a very Filipino book. I thought maybe, just maybe, there was a teeny bit of space in publishing for this brown Filipino author and her books featuring Filipino protagonists with dark skin and flat noses like hers.

Faith, Trust, and ~~Pixie Dust~~ Loving My Brown Skin

Having a fabulous agent on your side has its perks—you get to hone your writing craft with several rounds of editorial feedback. But best of all, Alyssa respected the Filipino-ness of my book, making sure it was still very much front and center as we made the plot better and more coherent.

This book was *My Fate According to the Butterfly*. We sold it to Scholastic. Before it was published, I did my first virtual author visit. I only had reviewer copies of my book back then, but I went through with it anyway since I wanted to do something to help promote my book.

The students I met virtually were from grades five to eight. The older kids occupied the second row, ready with their questions, while the younger ones hung farther back. Nobody wanted to sit in the front row, probably because they didn't want to stare at the projector screen with my face too close.

I remember seeing this small Asian girl at the back of the room, already looking bored before we even started. She was sitting beside a blond girl, who seemed more enthusiastic about hearing me talk. I guess she just got roped into attending my visit. Totally understandable—I once bought a book I had no interest in reading so I could accompany Isabelle to the book signing (the things we do for our friends).

Anyway, I started my virtual visit by introducing myself and *My Fate According to the Butterfly*. I brought my book up to the camera, making sure they saw the gorgeous cover in full glory. They showed their appreciation with oohs and aahs. But it was that kid, the bored little Asian kid at the back, who perked up in excitement. She popped out of her chair like a jack-in-the-box and took a seat in the empty front row.

I proceeded with the read-aloud while subtly keeping an eye on that girl. Up close, I could see she was Filipino American. I wasn't 100 percent sure, but considering the way she grinned at every mention of honorifics and Tagalog words peppered throughout . . . my gut told me this girl was Filipino like me.

Once I told the students they could go ahead and ask me questions, the girl was the first to raise her hand. She told me she was in the fifth grade, just like my main character, and she was super excited to read my book. Then she asked her question: "*Why* do you like ducks?"

I really had no idea why I like ducks (to this day, that's an existential question I still don't have an answer to), but she was satisfied with my simple "Because they are friendly animals" reply.

That was the first time I've ever experienced seeing a brown kid be excited over my book. It left me with so many feelings, in particular, the delight of knowing that I did something right with this book.

In the summer of 2019, I finally got to hold a finished hardcover copy of *My Fate According to the Butterfly*, with my sister by my side. We stopped filming the unboxing video before I got too emotional.

For my book launch, the Philippine team of Scholastic arranged a huge event with the whole media shebang. Readers and aspiring authors lined up to get my signature and have a photo with me. Kids imitated the expression of the brown Filipino girl on my cover, posing with the book held right next to their equally brown, happy faces. It seemed too amazing to be real. I had to pinch myself several times to remind myself I wasn't dreaming.

Sometime after, I came back to the bookstore I frequented as a kid. There, on the very shelf I browsed roughly twenty-six years ago, was a book with my name and a visibly brown, visibly flat-nosed Filipino girl on the cover.

It was surreal. I never would have thought my childhood dream could come true. But it did. It actually did.

Writing in Color

I eventually published my second book with Scholastic, *Sugar and Spite*. As of this writing, I'm in the process of working on a middle-grade fantasy series with HarperCollins, Lulu Sinagtala and the Tagalog Gods. I'm living my dream of becoming a published writer, initially fueled by rage and pain that eventually transformed into a desperate need to see myself in the books I read.

I'm not ashamed to admit I once hated the color of my skin. Part of the process of unlearning self-hate and self-devaluation is recognizing and accepting the reality of and the hurt from colorism. I needed to know and understand what I was up against before I could start dismantling the destructive message I'd internalized as a child. I had to learn to love my skin so I could write and share my truths as a Filipino author with a flat nose and a dark brown complexion.

I'll be honest and say the journey remains difficult for non-white authors like us. And it will probably continue to do so. Though our stories are no longer automatically shunned simply because our main characters aren't white, there will always be people who will insist on upholding the racist norm, people who will make us feel like we're just wasting our time on a dream that may never—and shouldn't ever—become reality.

But remember, there are also people who can see beyond prejudices. There are adults who will treasure our words and use them as beacons in their own journey to self-acceptance. There are teens who won't have to wait twenty-six years to realize that they matter, and that their stories are worth telling. There are kids who will be excited to know that they don't have to be sidekicks or villains all the time—they can be the heroes, too.

These people, our readers, young and old, are our little pockets of hope on a path that seems so difficult at every turn. They are the reason why we continue to fight this seemingly hopeless fight, making the journey worth every tear we shed and every crack that breaks our hearts.

Our readers are our pixie dust. But we are the fairies who weave stories that may one day become a lifeline to someone needing a reminder that they matter in times when their world is telling them they do not. Who cares if you're not the fairest fairy of them all? The world needs your voice, and we're all rooting for you.

Love your skin. Write your truths. Be unapologetically you.

Coping with Imposter Syndrome

BY JULIAN WINTERS

Julian Winters is the author of the IBPA Benjamin Franklin Gold Award–winning Running with Lions, *the Junior Library Guild Selections* How to Be Remy Cameron *and* The Summer of Everything, *and the multi-starred* Right Where I Left You. *A self-proclaimed comic book geek, Julian currently lives outside of Atlanta. He can usually be found swooning over rom-coms or watching the only two sports he can follow— volleyball and soccer. You can visit him online at julianwinters.com.*

In high school, there was an exclusive club for seniors. The 1000+ Club. The only entry requirement was for a student to score more than 1000 on their SATs. Induction included a T-shirt, special members-only meetings in the library, lunch with faculty, and an opportunity to be celebrated in front of your classmates.

A very distinguished honor.

The day of the introductory meeting, I remember my name being called over the loudspeakers. I got out of class early. Marched down the halls with my chin held high. I felt like I had something to be proud of. But when I walked in, silence and long stares greeted me.

I was the last one to arrive.

I was also the only Black boy in the room.

The first response from one of my peers was "Congratulations!" followed by "*You* got over 1000 on your SATs?" Then "What was your score?"

The club was made up of majority AP students. I'd known some of them since elementary school. They were mostly nice and friendly, but their questions signaled some-thing: I wasn't one of them.

I began to question: *How did I get here? Did they say the wrong name? Had the school confused me with someone else? Was it luck that I scored greater than 1000 on the test? Was I really as smart as I thought I was?* I didn't pull all-nighters studying. I was more concerned about acne and crushes than standardized tests. But I'd always been a great student. Not AP-worthy, but I rarely struggled with assignments. When I was called on by teachers, I knew the answers.

So how did I get in to this exclusive club where I was the only Black boy in the room?

At the time, I didn't have an answer for that question. I also never went back for the other meetings. Anxiety, doubt, and feeling like a fraud prevented me.

That day I made a new best friend—Imposter Syndrome.

While I'm certain there are other instances in my child-hood where this phenomenon truly took root, it was in that one moment—when my own classmates, the people I'd known since we were drinking juice boxes at lunch, made me feel like I didn't belong to a club I *earned* the right to be a part of—that paralyzing doubt truly blossomed.

Today, my Imposter Syndrome is a fully grown tree. Its thick branches often overshadow my accomplishments. Its strong trunk whispers questions all the time:

Am I worthy?

Do I belong here?

How much longer can I fool others into believing in me?

You would think as an author with four published novels,

multiple short stories (including one featured in a *New York Times*-bestselling book) in anthologies, a shiny and beautiful award for my debut novel, a handful of starred reviews, and a heaping of love from readers and authors alike, I'd be over feeling like a fraud. That I'd walk tall into every room, never lacking confidence. Unfortunately, that's not the case. Imposter Syndrome is a very real, often daunting phenomenon that can stick with you throughout every step of your journey, especially when you're a person of color still trying to figure out if you've earned your seat at the table.

Spoiler alert: *you have; get comfy.*

What is this dark, persistent voice in our heads that haunts our every thought of being successful? Why can't we own our accomplishments like others do?

Imposter Syndrome is loosely defined as the fear of being viewed as a fraud (particularly after achieving some form of professional success) that leads to the doubting of one's abilities. The concept was originally developed in the 1970s by psychologists Pauline Rose Clance and Suzanne Imes. Their study focused solely on high-achieving women. What wasn't included in their initial study was the impact of classism, xenophobia, professional background, the intersectionality of gender and ethnic background, and, of course, systemic racism, among other biases. While *everyone* is capable of experiencing Imposter Syndrome, intersectionality and environment are significant factors in the ways it affects someone.

Many high-profile celebrities have discussed their own battles with Imposter Syndrome. Depression, low self-esteem, anxiety. From Tom Hanks to Tina Fey to Lady Gaga. While touring for her book *Becoming*, former First Lady Michelle Obama openly talked about suffering from the phenomenon, despite being deeply respected by millions and holding one of the highest positions of power in the United States for eight years. It's also a title that had never been held by a person of color before.

Of course, this syndrome isn't limited to the people we see in front of cameras. Athletes, scholars, scientists. Even the chief executive officer of Starbucks, Howard Schultz, has discussed his struggles with it. There is no limit to where doubt can seed itself and grow.

In publishing, a business that is not known for employing and retaining non-white professionals on nearly every level, it's easy to fall into the trap of "I'm not as talented or competent as those surrounding me." How can you expect a "place at the table" when there are very few people seated that look or identify like you? The optics alone encourage second-guessing. The incessant feeling as if you're a magician and, someday soon, someone's going to see through your smoke and mirrors.

"What do you have under your hat?"

"What are you hiding up your sleeve?"

"Who's behind the curtain pulling the strings for you?"

Are you really talented and smart enough to make this a career?

There are a multitude of ways Imposter Syndrome manifests. For me, the most prominent is perfectionism. I see every flaw in my writing. I barely acknowledge my strengths, the things I do like no one else. More often than not, I'm comparing my first draft to someone's completed novel. *Why?* Because most of my life I've been told BIPOC individuals must be twice as good as anyone else just to receive equal respect. To earn their place.

My first attempt at writing needs to be as great as someone else's thoroughly edited, printed, and bound novel, otherwise I'm a fraud. I'm not as brilliant as them. I shouldn't be doing this.

Imagine having to throw a perfect touchdown like Tom Brady the first time you pick up a football. Being expected to hit a high note like Mariah Carey on your first attempt. Having to paint a *Mona Lisa* when you're still learning how to hold a brush.

It's not something you should *have to* do, but it's what Imposter Syndrome and systemic racism have told us as people of color.

Another way my Imposter Syndrome appears is my brain setting almost unreachable goals and feeling devastated when I immediately fail. Goals like becoming a *New York Times* bestseller with my debut novel. Being nominated and winning every literary award I'm eligible for. Drafting a deeply personal book in a short time. Going viral with my first TikTok.

(Yes, that last one was a real goal. It didn't happen.)

While some of these things *are* achievable, most aren't fully controlled by you. There are other external factors that come into play. You can't control trends, what people like or value as worthy, or even the weather. The problem is, Imposter Syndrome doesn't add those into the equation. It forces you to question your abilities when it takes two, three, maybe *fifteen times* to reach any of these goals.

My debut novel, *Running with Lions*, wasn't a *New York Times* bestseller. It wasn't shelved in every bookstore or library. But it won an award. It led me to meeting my dream literary agent when I was writing my *fourth* book. That deeply personal book? Despite Imposter Syndrome forcing me to overanalyze every word multiple times, it's now one of my most loved books by teachers, librarians, and young readers.

I haven't gone viral yet, but one step at a time.

The final way I'm affected by Imposter Syndrome is constantly working through everything alone. In some studies, this is called the Soloist. It's a need to isolate and not ask others for help for fear of them seeing weakness or incompetence in you. I do this often. It dates back to my 1000+ Club experience. Who hasn't been in class, terrified of being asked a question by the teacher because you don't want to be wrong in front of everyone? Even when you studied. You did the assignment. *You know the answer*. It's all right there and yet . . . you stay silent.

This feeling extends to publishing and being creative as well. The strong pull not to offer insight during a discussion you're knowledgeable on. Never sharing your work with others because they might see a flaw. The fear they will discredit you when, in truth, they might find value, uniqueness, and potential in not only your writing, but also your expertise.

Writing in Color

Unfortunately, Imposter Syndrome still makes you believe all of the above isn't enough.

You are not enough.

Imposter Syndrome can manifest in other ways. While it adversely affects people of color as a whole, every individual's experience is different. Remember: *we are not a monolith.* However, the fear, anxiety, and questioning remain constant in our communities.

How do we combat it, though? Here are a few tips I utilize:

Let yourself fail. The perfectionist in me hates this one. Is failure an option? Ask any of your non-BIPOC peers. The response might surprise you. Maybe it won't. Allow your first drafts to be messy. Apply for something you might not get. Say yes unapologetically to things you want to try. Write outside of your wheelhouse. Share an idea you'd love to pursue with an agent, editor, educator . . . or just a friend. Ask questions, even if you're unsure how to word them. Don't look at failure as confirmation of what Imposter Syndrome wants to tell you. Use failure as an opportunity to learn. As a reminder you're capable of growing. You haven't reached your final form.

Next: *Uplift other voices.* Specifically other people of color. In order to eliminate the feeling of "not belonging," I make room for more marginalized people. Imposter Syndrome tells you, "There is limited seating at the table." "There's only room for one [Insert Marginalization Here], and the rest of you have to wait outside." More lies. Elevating voices from inside our community allows us to *see* the ample space at the table. It also discredits the voices telling each of us that, despite our accomplishments, we haven't earned our spots.

Guess what? We're talented. We *deserve* to be here.

Another tip: if social media exacerbates your doubt or feelings of fraudulence, *limit it*. We're all guilty of using social media to flaunt our "best lives" at some point or another. Why show off the disappointments when I can talk about a new book deal? My shiny cover? *Look at me on the beach, not me slumped at my desk, questioning my life choices!* It's easy to fall into a dark hole of *Am I good enough?* when everything you see looks like the complete opposite of what you're experiencing. It's especially hard when a majority of those "success stories" aren't from other BIPOC. Here's something I remind myself of constantly: if it's not fun or motivating, it's not required. Log off. Set social media aside. Let it be something you turn to for entertainment and inspiration, not as a tool to assess your worth.

Little reminders help. One of the best ways to deal with Imposter Syndrome is to reread a chapter, scene, opening paragraph, single sentence you absolutely loved writing. Now read it again. One more time. Sink into that memory of when nothing could stop you from telling the story. Look at a first draft versus a third draft. Pinpoint the things you've accomplished. Collect emails and messages with positive feedback from people you've shared your work with. That note from your mom about a scene where she LOL'd so loud, she scared the cat? Save that, too. Hang these encouragements in a place where you can see them while working. One of the reasons doubt is able to linger for so long is because we have no evidence to disprove the things it's saying. But your words have power—allow yourself to look at their impact.

Reward yourself. Everyone knows the "Treat Yo Self" segment from *Parks and Recreation.* (If not, go watch it. Now.) While Retta's and Aziz Ansari's performances are hilarious beyond words, the lesson stands true. One of the best ways to combat Imposter Syndrome is to celebrate your accomplishments. For every milestone, big and small, you should reward yourself. Go for a long walk. Have some ice cream. Purchase a nice notebook or pen. Finally get that sweater you've been eyeing. Shout about it on the internet. This doesn't solely apply to the major milestones either. The minor accomplishments are just as important. Doubt thrives on our failures. The things we leave unfinished because fear talked us out of seeing them through. Rewarding yourself allows you to look back at the bridges crossed, the hills climbed, the risks taken, and say, "I can do it again," when faced with your next goal.

Own it. Easier said than done, right? As people of color, most of us were taught to work extra hard to earn and *maintain* our spots. Systemic racism and biases tell us, "Keep your head down. Do what you're supposed to. It's the only way." The unreasonable demands and expectations not applied to our white counterparts lead us to stay silent about our fear of failure amongst peers. We're afraid it'll be looked at as complaining. The moment we speak out, we're labeled as "difficult" or "incapable" or "in over our heads." Imposter Syndrome at its finest. I encourage you to openly discuss these thoughts with people you trust. Friends, other BIPOC peers, a therapist. You'll be amazed at how many others will confess to feeling the same way. Even as I write this essay, Imposter Syndrome asks in its haunting echo, "Who are you to talk about this? Do you know enough about this topic to help anyone?"

And you know what? I do. *You* do. We're stronger in numbers. We silence doubt by raising our voices.

There are several other methods to coping with Imposter Syndrome that I encourage you to explore: (1) Positive affirmations—tell your reflection or record yourself saying affirming things about yourself. Play it back when you're feeling doubtful. (2) Own every success—you didn't reach this point by luck. By chance. There was no mistake when they called your name for an award or prize. *You* played a significant role in your accomplishments. Be proud. Tell others. (3) Visualize future success. Imagine yourself writing the book. Passing that test. Finishing the race. Being in front of an audience talking about your work. Signing your first finished novel. Standing tall at the end. Build confidence in yourself before going after something. Cut the root of uncertainty out before it ever has an opportunity to bloom.

As hindering as dealing with Imposter Syndrome can be, I've also learned to use it as a motivator. I find ways to challenge that little voice in my head. I meet the "You're not good enough to write that" with "I am. Watch me." Every "There's no room for your voice here" is swatted away with

Writing in Color

an "If there isn't space, I'll make it for myself." If my mind says, "Will anyone want to read this?" I remind myself that when I was younger, *I* needed it. The book, the plot, the characters, the perspective of someone like me. There's never "enough," especially when you haven't had the opportunity to tell your version of a story.

To be fair, I didn't achieve this confidence overnight. Over the years, I've built a community of authors I can talk my feelings through with. Slacks, group chats, Discords, texts, a Zoom call or two. But I also have supportive friends and family and the occasional online message from a former classmate who's proud of me. Your greatest ally against any fears is having people you can turn to when uncertainty creeps in. You need a team of not only knowledgeable people, but also ones that will break out the pom-poms and cheer you on.

At the inception of this essay, I hadn't realized how long I'd been dealing with this imposter phenomenon. All the insidious ways it has skewed my views. The hesitation toward things I *knew* I could achieve. Decades of microaggressions, expectations, second-guessing my worth. I allowed it to fester in the darkest places of my brain.

If I could go back to that first 1000+ Club meeting, I'd walk in with more swagger. I wouldn't answer questions about what my score was. I wouldn't flinch at the condescending "*You* got over 1000 on your SATs?"

Instead, I'd say, "I'm here. I belong. I'm as brilliant as you. Also, can you move over? You're in *my* seat."

I hope this essay has helped you understand Imposter

Syndrome a little better. I hope you've found ways to cope with it. As people of color, I don't know if we ever "overcome" the doubt or fear or feeling like a fraud. At least, I haven't. But we can fight it. We can claim our rightful places at the table. A difficult but powerful lesson I've learned throughout my life is that there's always room; you just have to be brave enough to take the first step.

Remember: Imposter Syndrome can't exist without you first achieving some form of success. It can't plant the seed unless you've made an effort to go after your dreams. Don't hesitate. Don't overanalyze. Don't let others devalue your worth or brilliance. You don't owe it to anyone to be perfect. You don't have to be an overachiever. You don't have to know everything.

You simply have to try.

This is where you're supposed to be.

You belong.

Writing in Color

The Care and Keeping of Jealousy

BY KARUNA RIAZI

Karuna Riazi is a born and raised New Yorker, with a loving, large extended family and the rather trying experience of being the eldest sibling in her particular clan. She holds a BA in English literature from Hofstra University and an MFA in writing for children and young adults from Hamline University's MFAC program, and she is an educator and online diversity advocate. She is the middle-grade author of The Gauntlet *(S&S/Salaam Reads, 2017),* The Battle *(S&S/Salaam Reads, 2019), and* A Bit of Earth *(Greenwillow Books, 2023).*

You've probably already paused.

Stopped there, in your tracks, by the title of this entry.

"The care and keeping of jealousy?"

Because, of course, like so many others, you have been taught that your jealousy is an ugly, foul thing.

It is a creature that never dies—a zombie, possibly, for all the blows you fling toward it never seem to be the killing blow.

Or, better yet, a vampire: darkly seductive, sickening and charming at once with its whispers of *Why can't it be you?*

Why isn't it you?

How could this person who isn't you deserve this?

You shut it away in its coffin and hope no one can see the puncture wounds where you've injured yourself—through self-doubt, self-recrimination, self-loathing—in order to nurture hate and suspicion and bitterness.

And, if someone does reach out and fling back the lid—

"You're jealous, aren't you?"

Shame.

Shame, and guilt, and more self-loathing. How could you keep this festering away? How could this awful, awful feeling be revealed to others, and what must they think of you?

They must be judging you.

They must think badly of you.

Because good people aren't jealous.

And jealousy is never good.

But "jealousy is never good, and you're not a good person because you're jealous" is not a good take.

It ignores why we, as authors of color and from marginalized identities and experiences, may feel jealousy, and the very real fears and concerns that jealousy indicates that should not be trod upon, dismissed, or degraded.

And most importantly, this take—this taught indoctrination that your negative emotions are shameful, ugly, and a deeper indicator of your lack of goodness and worth as a person—was designed to ignore all that history and only worsen the problems of jealousy.

Short, in-a-nutshell summary?

Jealousy as we view, experience, and dismiss it now as authors of color is rooted firmly in white supremacy.

But, wait a minute.

How?

Yes, white supremacy has poisoned a lot of how we perceive, write, and present ourselves to the world—but internally to this extent?

What does white supremacy have to do with that bitter

knot in your stomach when an acquaintance gushes about their new agent on Twitter?

Bear with me. We're getting there.

Let's break it down this way.

We work within publishing, which is an established system that—like all established systems in the Western world—functions with white supremacy as its primary anchor and means of viewing the world.

Marginalized lives, voices, and experiences are valued, protected, and uplifted last.

If at all.

We like to think we're constantly conscious of that—and in some ways, we are.

I know I am.

I know that every single time I put finger to keyboard, arm myself with all the right buzzwords—"trendy, timely, on brand"—to similarly aid my agent in her campaign to ensure that I, as much as my latest manuscript, can be appealingly marketable to editors, the barriers ahead of me are front and center in my mind.

Not just the acquisitions room, or the marketing team, but beyond: sales, and awards, and avoiding the many ways in which the world continues to try and silence our voices and our stories, from book bans to curated bestseller lists.

But being conscious of it doesn't always mean being aware of how it affects us—not just through the mental strain of preparing for rejections that are coyly bigoted ("I couldn't connect with your character!" or "We already have our XYZ character/author/vague presence for the season/

next season/all of eternity"), but how we internalize the messages this institution gives us about ourselves and use them not only to judge our worth but also that of our peers.

In an industry where we're constantly taught both "It's not you" and "It's subjective, so that means that something about you just didn't work for me," it doesn't take too long to go from "What's wrong with me?" to "What's so great about them?"

And we try so very hard not to feel that way.

We do.

I know I do.

I know you do too.

But you can't help but feel that way when you've been taught this myth of scarcity, that publishing can only reserve a certain number of seats per demographic, that you need to do whatever you can to claw your way into that seat and—

Once you have it—

Make sure no one else can get it from you.

And sometimes, that ugly, swarming mass inside us—it whispers for us to go one step farther, maybe one step too far, from clicking away from Rights Report or not being able to force a congratulations out to the latest success story or just bitterly rolling your eyes when no one else can see you.

Maybe it's not wanting to share someone else's name in a room of opportunity, or singling out a marginalized author of your same background with catty gossip and sup-position that they aren't "XYZ enough" (not like you are)—because what if they are liked more, what if this seat that doesn't quite fit you is the only seat you'll ever be offered, what if they are more talented, what if this means you will be entirely forgotten and overlooked and unwanted and unpublished for all of eternity?

Maybe toppling their chances will increase yours.

Except it doesn't.

Except that you both are enough and can be enough, and deserve seats at the same table without yanking the chair between you so that both of you plummet to the ground.

What makes you feel that isn't true?

What makes us feel so panicked when a friend's idea is just a hair too close to our latest magnum opus (even if logically, "They all look the same/their stories sound the same" biases aside, they really don't), when we should feel excited for them and for all of us to have more comp titles and comrades within the same genres to bolster panels and roundtables and reading advisory selections?

It's white supremacy. It lies.

And we take in the lies, and as much as we think we aren't holding to them, being told them enough makes them feel like the truth.

But, if this is all centuries of colonization and said colonization's control of our stories and voices and indoctrinated bigotry yet again rearing its ugly head, why am I encouraging you to take care of it and tend it, instead of yank it up by its roots and cast it over your shoulder without a glance back?

Because white supremacy is part of jealousy, but not completely.

It explains our particular jealousy as experienced within

the context of publishing—and how we must push back on it in order to destabilize and ultimately destroy it, rather than each other, and make a more powerful, unified effort to lift each other higher—but not why we feel it to begin with.

The truth is, jealousy is a painfully normal, inherent human trait.

Yes, understanding that we're not entirely responsible for this panic, this fear, this sense of futility in pursuing publication for our art because there's always someone who seems to be getting it all while we try to make a feast for our emotions out of crumbs, is why I point out the importance of holding white supremacy accountable and culpable.

But I suspect we would still feel those twinges—if not on a constant basis—without it.

As humans, we are hardwired to want: to be ambitious, to aspire.

It is a beautiful and horrible desire, because it never feels like we can quite satisfy it. And meanwhile, it appears that everyone else is just so much better—at wanting, at ambition, at going a step past aspiring into absolutely obtaining.

This is why we care for jealousy—because, like it or not, we must keep it.

We must recognize that the little twinge is not the curling of a monster's fingers around the edge of a coffin lid, but the slight unfurling of an occasionally dormant plant in our heart.

We must look to what has watered it, what has made it stir in our chest—a book deal, a movie release, a scroll

Writing in Color

through the gleaming highlights reel that is Instagram— and respect that our feeling does not indicate we are bad people.

Instead, it indicates we are frustrated, tired, in need of more than what we currently have, and assuming that someone else having what we think we need means either they are better than us or happier than us.

There is nothing bad about that: as long as we let the water flow away before it awakens the toxic thorns that lash out at other people, in anger, in undeserved scorn, in accusations—even if that means clicking away, moving back, taking a deep breath, saying congratulations, and then calling it a night to self-soothe and detox.

Prioritizing ourselves, and not letting the pricking of those thorns make us believe that we deserve the pain, is what is key to the care and keeping of jealousy.

At every turn, don't deprecate yourself or feel like you're being weak for having to tend it to this extent—for timing your social media exposure, for the nights when the ache is strong and you simply can't write and feel foolish for having wasted time later, for wondering if pursuing this dream is worth it at all.

If you let the water flow away from the thorns, aim it toward the root: the fear. Let those roots curl into the reassuring soil of your support—those who believe in you. Write that anxious email to a critique partner or agent if you must. Have long conversations with your therapist in which you explain every spare detail of the publishing process. Allow yourself to be reassured, praised, and loved on.

You are not a bad person. You deserve the encouragement. You deserve the acknowledgment of all the goodness, talent, and wonder in you that a white-supremacist institution is not equipped or often willing to see.

There is nothing foul about those moments when jealousy makes you feel small and shriveled inside.

Ugly?

Of course.

There is nothing beautiful about the systems that we are constricted by and that weigh so heavily on our sense of worth, muddling our art and our intentions with concerns about capitalism and making our trauma palatable enough to sell.

If there is any creature that is worth crushing with a killing blow, it is the structure that attempts to fool us into thinking our stories can be condensed into one slot for one lucky winner—and, in acknowledging our jealousy and tending it ourselves through acknowledging it, we continue to work toward that final blow.

In not letting it eat us alive—in giving it the occasional night or feeling of disappointment or good cry after a rejection, before straightening out our shoulders and launching ourselves into the words and stories that we can't let go of— we are fighting back.

By rejecting the desire of white supremacy for us to tear each other apart, rather than see someone else succeed where it feels we're currently failing (never failing, though— just in a state of transition not near our ultimate goal), we are weakening its defenses.

Writing in Color

And, by realizing that there is nothing wrong with our feeling jealousy at all, we're working toward a day when we might see it finally brought to its knees.

Short, in-a-nutshell summary?

You're jealous. And that's fine.

There's more to it than just being petty, or awful, or intrinsically flawed.

Good people can be jealous.

It's all about what you do with the jealousy—and how you move forward in spite of it.

Real Talk

BY YAMILE SAIED MÉNDEZ

Yamile Saied Méndez is the author of many books, including Furia, *a Reese's Book Club selection for YA and the winner of the inaugural Pura Belpré Young Adult Author Award. She was born and raised in Rosario, Argentina, but has lived most of her life in the US in a lovely valley surrounded by mountains with her family. An inaugural Walter Dean Myers Grant recipient, she is also a graduate of the Vermont College of Fine Arts. She's a founding member of Las Musas, a marketing collective of Latine authors.*

My first book, *Blizzard Besties*, came out at the end of 2018. By the time this anthology is published, I will have published more than twelve books and several short stories in multiple anthologies, with several others to come and under contract. Sometimes when I'm introduced, people call me an overnight success. The truth is that my journey started decades ago, and, as is the case with many writers, this path hasn't been smooth or easy.

There are so many things I wish I had known as a young aspiring writer, and I hope that in reading about my journey, you will find both inspiration and advice on things to look out for.

Through the years of my writer apprenticeship, I have learned that the public only sees the tip of the iceberg. The countless hours of work, the multiple rejections before and after becoming a published author, the heartbreak of a book not earning out or, worse, not reaching its readers, are private matters that don't make for popular social media posts. Hopefully my experience will motivate you, young dreaming writer, when you struggle with finding the time, support, or motivation to share your stories with the world.

When I was a small child in Argentina, I had two dreams: becoming a writer and being a mother. It might seem an oxymoron to feminists, but my mother was a working woman and she was the most amazing person I ever knew. I grew up seeing her juggle her jobs and her family, and although I knew it wasn't easy, I always wanted to have a family of my own. This wish was granted first.

I married young, and by the time I graduated college, I already had a little baby. At twenty-nine years old, I was already the mother of four children under the age of six. My husband had a very demanding job, and he traveled frequently. Although I worked outside the home at the beginning of our marriage, soon, I became the main caretaker of our family. I loved the opportunity to stay at home with my children.

They're my pride and joy.

In those early years, I worked as a freelance translator and interpreter, and when circumstances allowed it, the children and I joined my husband where his job took him. From small towns in Virginia and Missouri, to Florida and southern Texas, the first places I looked up were the town library and the local independent bookshops. Very much like with the mother in the book *Dreamers* by Yuyi Morales, the library became our refuge and place of inspiration. In college I studied international economics, but I never forgot my early dream of one day becoming an author. During our visits to the library, I fantasized about seeing my name on

Writing in Color

the cover of a book one day, visiting readers, signing my name on much-read and -loved books.

Spanish is my first language, and the writing conventions in English are very different from what I had learned growing up. Also, although I read *Little Women* and *Heidi* as a child, I wasn't familiar with the American canon of children's literature. I discovered the world of Clifford the Big Red Dog, Max and his Wild Things, Matilda, and Junie B. Jones along with my children. Every day, they'd come home from preschool and share with me the books the teachers read aloud, and the nursery rhymes I hadn't grown up with.

I absorbed these stories into my soul.

Reading was my doorway into the world of American children's literature. Soon, I wanted to share my stories with my children and other young readers too. But I knew no other aspiring writers of my background. Back then, we lived in a small town in Utah. Before social media, it was difficult to connect with other writers and learn how to find an agent and eventually publish a book. But I found other like-minded people who became my first critique group, and more than that, dear friends. However, none of them spoke or wrote in Spanish or in a language that wasn't their mother tongue, for that matter.

Although the story I was writing (which one day would be known as my young adult debut, *Furia*) was set in Argentina, I realized that if I wanted to tell that story, I'd have to write it in English.

In the early 2000s, there weren't any books in the mainstream market with titles in Spanish, but this was the story of my heart, and I studied all the elements of craft that would help me do this story justice. Not for the first time, I became frustrated that the day only had twenty-four hours and they weren't enough.

Just like when I was in high school (studying English for the TOEFL and the SAT, and trying to balance school, work, and a social life), I had to get creative with how I managed my time.

I wrote my story during my children's nap times. I stayed up until the wee hours of the night, many times with a little one strapped in a baby sling while I typed with one hand. My children were used to seeing me lugging my laptop along or a notebook to jot down the ideas that would assail me at the most inconvenient places, like during the car-pool pickup time. I had the lightning-bolt idea of my first picture book, *Where Are You From?*, waiting for my son's favorite author to sign his book.

After several years of meeting monthly with my critique group, I started sending out my story to agents and editors (in a query letter). I received so much wonderful feedback and compliments about the writing voice and style, about the themes and characterization. But in the end, they invariably commented that they didn't know how to market my book, or that they already had another Latina author on their list. Even if that Latina author was of a very different background than me or wrote very different stories from mine.

I'm an optimistic person, but by then, I had started assessing my plan. I came to the conclusion that if I contin-

Writing in Color

ued doing the same thing, I would have the same result—a form rejection letter.

It was the time to change tactics. During a writing workshop, I found out about a writing program in Vermont. It seemed a paradise for writers with busy lives like mine. It was a low-residency master's program that accommodated writers who had families or jobs and couldn't move to attend a regular master's course. At the time, my oldest child was fourteen years old, and my youngest was only two. My husband's job didn't require so much travel anymore. At night, while my family slept and after I'd achieved my word count of the day, I browsed the school website, fantasizing about being part of this program.

I considered myself a brave person. After all, I'd moved by myself from Argentina to the United States at age nineteen to attend college. I arrived in Provo, Utah, where I knew no one. Although I had studied English all my life, I struggled to understand English in a college setting. But I had graduated even when I had a small baby. I had proved to myself that I could do difficult things.

However, there were so many more factors to consider this time. One of my children struggled with depression and anxiety, another had major life-threatening allergies, and my youngest was only a toddler. My husband encouraged me to apply, to give it a shot. I was accepted as part of the cohort of winter 2015. I was thrilled, but also very scared and worried.

Although I had lived in Utah for a long time, I wasn't used to Vermont's negative-thirty-degree weather. I was worried about how my children, dogs, and husband (in that order! Ha!) would cope without me. I was scared that I wouldn't have the skills to keep up with my classmates. I feared that the administrators would call me aside and tell me there had been a mistake and my acceptance had been revoked.

Later, I would learn that this was my undiagnosed anxiety messing with my emotions. I'm glad that my happiness and enthusiasm for learning from admired mentors and being inspired by my classmates were stronger than my fears.

On the flight home, however, the fears resurfaced. It had been relatively easy to keep up with the lectures and workshops during the residency, but how would I cope when I was home and there wasn't a cafeteria to provide three meals a day?

The monthly workload (forty pages of creative work, two critical essays, a bibliography of at least ten books to read and analyze) seemed insurmountable if I added housework, childcare, and freelance work. (I was a sensitivity reader or cultural consultant for several publishers.)

I would have to withdraw from the program, even if having to make this decision was excruciating to me.

Once again, my husband was the voice of reason. He suggested that I continue with the semester. After all, we had already paid the tuition, which was nonrefundable.

I gave it a try.

But first, I had to get a system. Thankfully, my older four children were attending school full-time, and my youngest was in a morning preschool program. Although I have always been a notorious night owl, I changed my schedule so that I could wake up at five in the morning, to get a couple of hours of writing time before my children woke up for school. After the morning car pool, I set out three hours of more work, stopping at noon when my little one got out of preschool. After lunch, he and I read picture books. During car pools to dance lessons and sports, we listened to audiobooks. In the evenings, we all sat down to do our homework.

Looking back, the two years in which our whole family was devoted to my education sound idyllic. But there were medical emergencies, the loss of a beloved dog, challenging incidents of racism and discrimination at my son's school during a heated presidential campaign, and a period of deep depression the likes of which I hadn't experienced since a bout of postpartum depression after my first son was born. But like the popular slogan at the time said, *I persisted.*

In January 2017, on the day of an emotionally charged presidential inauguration, I finally graduated with my class. My children and husband were cheering for me in the audience. My agent cheered while watching the livestream online. I had crested the wave I'd been riding for two years.

I didn't want to plummet to the depths of the depression that had been pulling me down for more than a year. As I had done throughout my life, I tried to manage my frustrations, fears, and concerns through work, or staying busy. In fact, many times I joked that writing was my therapy, even when I was working on happy stories. I continued the neckbreaking pace of rising before the sun to get a couple of hours of uninterrupted working time before my children woke up. The system worked for a while. By then, I had several books under contract. It was time to implement all the lessons I had learned during my master's program.

"If you don't stop, your body stops for you," my mother used to say when she was alive. It was more a reminder for herself than for me since she never followed her own advice. My mother died from a heart attack at age fifty-four, leaving us devastated.

Although she had been gone for three years already, her words resonated in my mind as I struggled to fulfill my obligations.

The system of working relentlessly while also being a full-time parent was taking a heavy toll on me. My health started deteriorating and soon, the symptoms started showing up in my writing. My stories lacked . . . something. Even if my critique group was enthusiastic, and my agent and editor told me everything was okay, I felt something was missing. That spark that had guided me through so many years wasn't there anymore.

But the book that I had started writing when my children were babies had finally sold to the publishing house and editor of my dreams. Not only that, it had also been selected by a celebrity book club, shattering all my expectations.

It's redundant to state that the year 2020 was a very difficult year for humanity as a whole, but with two books close to my heart (*On These Magic Shores* and *Furia*) coming out during the worst of the pandemic, I started wondering if all the work, effort, and sacrifice had been worth it.

Writing in Color

I have always been a spiritual person, if not always necessarily religious. The oldest child of four, I was a quiet child who had a rich, loud inner life. The way in which I chose to express the whirlwind inside me was through writing. I felt too much, and it hurt. Grief, loneliness, frustration? I couldn't just point at those words and say that's what I felt, but I could find a way around them and put them in a story that would help myself understand what it was that I felt. And when I couldn't express myself through writing, at least I could find a mirror in my beloved books that I read and reread until the pages fell apart.

During 2020, I didn't have words to express my emotions. What's even worse, I didn't find comfort in reading, either.

I had only experienced this kind of disconnection from words twice before: when my last baby was in the hospital fighting for his life, and when my mom died.

This time, however, I had professional commitments to fulfill. Virtual events replaced a much-expected book tour, and even when my family was struggling with the loss of family members to Covid, I still had to sign in and smile on camera for the supportive readers who showed up for my book and me.

During the months after *Furia* came out, in different interviews, I was asked how or why I became a writer. Many times, I talked about how I started writing in third grade, after my beloved grandfather passed away. Even then, I processed my emotions through writing.

But when I consider what inspired me to write in the

first place, the first thing that comes to mind is that although Argentina is known for its beef, and rock en español, and Eva Perón, Che Guevara, Pope Francis, and of course, fútbol, or soccer, we're also known for our love of stories and books.

I was born in Rosario, Argentina, in 1977, during one of the most brutal periods of a military dictatorship that created such incredible trauma, my country is still trying to process it and deal with its aftereffects. One of the first things the new democratic president, Raúl Alfonsín, did was commission the gathering of the stories of the thirty thousand who'd disappeared and those who'd suffered persecution, and make a book. Ernesto Sábato, the famed novelist, was in charge of the task, and they called the book *Nunca Más*. Never again.

It's been more than forty years, and with the benefit of time and distance from my country, I've been learning how to process the collective trauma that El Proceso de Reorganización Nacional[2] left in my DNA.

Just as I was a child who dealt with trauma through writing, I've always been a very motivated individual. Maybe because watching the Argentine soccer team win the World Cup in Mexico in 1986 left me with a desire to get a gold medal and make my family proud. But as I've also said during my many events for *Furia*, soccer wasn't a viable path for me. Not because my parents were horrible people that didn't let me pursue my passions. Quite the opposite. They saw my passion for story was more viable, and so they

2 The Process of National Reorganization

Writing in Color

encouraged me to receive the best education they could give me. My dad was a taxi driver, and my mom a house cleaner and nanny, but they tried their best so I could go to school and learn English.

Seeing their faith in me and their immense sacrifice, I saw it was my duty as a daughter and as a human to use all my talents to improve my life and help my family and the world.

I set goals.

They weren't like the goals my brothers had scored on a soccer field, but my family celebrated with me as the first one who graduated high school, learned English, and was accepted to a US university! It's hard for people who see me now to calculate how impossible it was for me, a poor girl from public housing, to arrive in the US on a student visa to go to school. Sometimes I think about how the odds were stacked against me, and I marvel at how we did it.

It was a family effort, but I still had to do the work. Fueled with their support, trust, and faith, I had to put in the effort. It was then that I learned to set goals.

My goals had helped me through my master's program, and the victory of finding a publisher for my books. But now, when my health started suffering, I realized that I had neglected to set spiritual, mental, emotional, and physical goals too.

And this time, my usual methods of being productive didn't work.

I lit candles, played instrumental music, bought different journals and planners that remained empty, made a plan with my best friend to be accountability partners, made declarations on social media to keep myself accountable to sitting in front of my computer. And I was productive. But . . . my heart wasn't really in the words. Writing didn't bring me the joy or emotional release I had always counted on. The spark wasn't there.

Why?

Why was I suffering through my first major writer's block? The world was going through a pandemic. And I wasn't able to visit my family abroad even when a beloved aunt passed away. But I had the luxury of working from home. My children and husband were healthy.

Things were going great with *Furia* even with so many odds against it.

I had nothing to complain about in my life.

But then, a good friend noted that when I spoke with her, I was holding my breath between sentences.

Without breath, my stories didn't have life.

I knew it. I felt it as I revised my stories. My words didn't have emotions because I was afraid of feeling them.

I had repressed those emotions for so long, however, that I didn't know how to tap into them anymore. My friend suggested I go to a yoga class with a sound bath. She was certain that the sound of the gongs would unblock my emotions. And she was right. That day, I had announced the eighth book my agent sold that year, and I was happy to go to yoga and celebrate. During the sound bath, I had my first panic attack in more than three decades.

It was the strongest call for help my body had sent me.

Writing in Color

If I didn't take care of my mental, emotional, and physical health, then there wouldn't be a viable medium for the stories my heart had to tell.

It seems simple, but the first things that helped me become healthy again were simple too: exercise, time in nature, nutritious meals, and learning how to say no. This last item has been the hardest one on my list. I have so many ideas and hopes for those ideas, but there is only one me and, unfortunately, the day only has twenty-four hours.

It's a continuous process, but I have had to learn to prioritize my physical and mental health. But the most important thing has been learning how to live in the present, inside my body, even when my emotions are uncomfortable.

I still love being my children's mother even though I had four teenagers at a time. Their lives are theirs to live, and I'm honored to be part of them. Being a mother has been an opportunity to see the world anew with each child.

They're the reason I finally got the courage to pursue my dream of becoming a published author. Now that my books are published, I receive countless messages from readers, of all ages and backgrounds, sharing what the words born from my emotions meant to them. Now these readers are the reason I write too.

When things are difficult, I remember why I write. I remember my young self, sitting in front of a Spanish/English dictionary, trying to gather enough building blocks to eventually create my stories.

These reasons give me the power to write even through difficult situations. Finding my why is what connects me to the rest of creation, to other people, nature, divinity.

Time and again, I'm reminded that writing is a journey and that the goal isn't a specific destination.

The accolades, awards, and praise come and go. But the most precious moments have been in front of my laptop or notebook, when an idea grabs me by the scruff of my neck, or when it whispers quietly in my ear.

Writing is how I witness the preciousness and difficulty of this journey we call life. Because what are we storytellers if not the witnesses of life?

Writing in Color

Perseverance

BY DARCIE LITTLE BADGER

Darcie Little Badger is a Lipan Apache writer with a PhD in oceanography. Her critically acclaimed novels, Elatsoe *and* A Snake Falls to Earth, *were national Indie Bestsellers and have received numerous awards, including a Newbery Honor. Darcie is married to a veterinarian named Taran.*

Frequently, I get the question, "What advice would you give somebody who wants to be a writer?" That's a tricky one. What works for me might not work for you, and even if it does, what works for us might not work for anyone else. For example, when it comes to first drafts, I'm what they call a "pantser," as in "by the seat of my pants." An idea pops into my head, and I start writing, eager to learn where the story will take me. Did I plan the essay you're currently reading? Sorta, yeah. Mentally. It shape-shifted a few times between drafts number one and number two, but that's all part of the process.

On the other hand, my good friend methodically fills entire journals with plot points, character descriptions, and world-building notes before she'll even consider starting chapter one of a new book. Both of us are authors. Neither of us is "right" or "wrong." Creation's personal, you know?

But while I cannot offer people a universal tip for success as a writer, I can describe my own writing journey—

including the greatest lesson I've ever learned—with the sincere hope that it'll be helpful.

Starting from the beginning, I've wanted to be a writer since before I could write; my first attempted books were chaotic scribbles on construction paper. See, Mom and Dad raised me in a home full of stories. They'd read from picture books and recite Mother Goose poetry; Dad recounted funny incidents in his life; Mom told the traditional legends of our people. I quickly learned that stories are vessels of entertainment, understanding, and knowledge; they change every person they touch. And that power fascinated me.

Although I was born in Minnesota (thankfully, given my dislike of cold winters, we didn't stay there long), my parents initially met each other, fell in love, and got married in Texas. That said, their histories have very different roots.

Dad was the second child in a large Irish American family; he was raised in Seguin and would always have a slight Texas accent, no matter where he moved. By all accounts, my father was a considerate, good-humored child and an exceptionally responsible, hardworking young man. Aspiring to be a teacher, Dad paid for college by painting houses, working in a steel mill, and doing construction for the city of Seguin. He also found time to star as the iconic vampire in a dramatic performance of *Dracula*. The college newspaper took a photo of him in costume, wearing a cape and sharp teeth and looking so young, I barely recognize him, although there's no mistaking his smile.

In his youth, my dad was known for his wit, which

Writing in Color

sharpened with age, and his intelligence, which evolved into a quiet, empathetic wisdom.

Well, Mom was the third child in a large Lipan Apache family. Born in McAllen, Texas, she lived near the US-Mexico border, which cuts through our traditional homeland. As a girl, Mom read all the sci-fi books in the local library. She'd dream about space and play with the wrenches in my grandpa's toolbox, imagining that they were aliens. That must've amused him. According to those who knew him, Grandpa was a jokester with a bottomless cache of funny stories. I wish I could have heard some. But Grandpa was killed in an accident when Mom was just fourteen. Throughout her teen years, she helped raise her siblings, the family barely surviving in conditions of extreme poverty. Nevertheless, determined to become a scientist, Mom finished high school, got accepted to Pan American University, and then jogged to college three times a week, her books carried in a backpack (before backpacks were cool). Since college was thirteen miles away from home, this phase of life transformed my mother into an accidental marathon runner. But she still had enough remaining energy to earn a degree in biology.

In her youth, my mom was a flame, and her fire has grown only brighter with time.

As for me? Like I said: my parents raised me in a home full of stories, and those stories encouraged me to tell my own.

After I learned the alphabet and started elementary school, my next attempted books were handwritten in Lisa Frank journals; for anyone born in the twenty-first century, I should explain that Lisa Frank—a designer of neon rainbow accessories with lots of happy animals—was a phenomenon in the nineties, just like Beanie Babies and colorful gel pens. Notably, one of my unfinished books is titled *The Quest for Beanie Babies*; the less said about it, the better, but I can confirm that it was written with a lime-green gel pen. I also penned a thriller about a school fire; it was titled *Sometimes Change Is Good*, but because I never finished the book, I can't remember what the good part was supposed to be.

The first paragraph of *Sometimes Change Is Good* (early 1990s), including all original spelling and grammatical errors:

> Fire was everywhere. My name is Tina and I never
> thought this would happen. Today begun like
> any other day, but it is ending way different. It
> all started during math. We were talking about
> divition like all schools do. I was listening to
> my teacher, Mrs. Kay, when a loud bell went of.
> Every-one looked up.

Initially, I wrote entirely for myself 'cause it was fun, like playing games of make-believe played across colorful sheets of paper. You can be a writer for an audience of one. Nothing wrong with that. But I increasingly wondered: Could my stories make other people happy too? What would it take to see my name on library shelves, among my favorite authors?

My first completed novel was a forty-page mystery about a murdered garden, a mysterious bag of opals, and the girl who investigated the secrets in her neighborhood. I typed it on the family Macintosh, which—in those early days of personal computers—was mostly good for word processing and Tetris. At the time, my parents were graduate students, so they needed the computer; in fact, Dad was writing a four-hundred-page dissertation on the Elizabethan poet Christopher Marlowe. Still, they patiently gave me permission to type my book, letter by careful letter, over a period of months.

Finally, after typing "The End" in *Murdered Garden Mystery*[3], I printed it for my parents, who'd agreed to be its first—but hopefully not last—readers. Aware that I wanted to get *Murdered Garden Mystery* published, Dad read my manuscript front to back, and then—in between his work, his research, and his responsibilities to our family—edited my book with a bright red pen. To be completely clear: I was seven years old. My first-grade class was still learning basic grammar and spelling. So Dad had his work cut out for him, but not only did he edit every page, he also explained the edits, teaching me how to process content-related and grammatical feedback. Then he went a step further. Once I was satisfied with draft number two of *Murdered Garden Mystery*, Dad helped me write a query letter[4], and we sent my manuscript to a genuine publisher.

---

3 The actual title was probably more creative.

4 A "query letter" is an introduction you send to an agent or editor when you want them to help publish your book. It should be brief and make them interested in reading your project. To paraphrase my earliest query letter: *Dear Editor, I am a small child from Iowa, USA. Will you please consider my debut novel for publication? Thank you for your time and consideration. Sincerely, Darcie*

The response was a prompt (but very kind) rejection letter.

Look, it's rarely fun to get rejected. However, I don't recall feeling all too bad about my first professional setback. No doubt that's 'cause Dad insisted I should be proud, not discouraged. In fact, he framed the rejection letter. It was proof that I'd taken a difficult, important step in my journey. Someday, he said, when I published my first book, the letter would remind me how far I'd come, how hard I'd worked to achieve my dream. Until then, he said, keep writing.

It's a good lesson to learn early. It's no secret that authors deal with lots of rejection, and the playing field isn't always level. The more I read, the more I noticed discrepancies between the stories that traditional publishing favored and the Indigenous stories I'd grown up with.

In many ways, I'm like my mother. For example, we're both major fans of sci-fi and fantasy. The first book Mom bought—just a kid, she got it for one nickel at a library sale—tells the adventures of a fairy named Poppy. Although its cover is now tattered, and its pages are more delicate than butterfly wings, the old book sits on a shelf alongside our family photo albums. As a voracious young reader, I also found solace among the "genre" shelves of libraries and bookstores.

However, of the hundreds of science fiction and fantasy (SFF) books I consumed between first and twelfth grade, none had a Native American protagonist, and zero mentioned the Lipan Apache. We didn't even exist in the background. Heck, I went to high school in Texas, the traditional homeland of my people, but we were even absent from the history textbooks.[5]

Generally, I enjoy reading about characters who are different than me. It would be extremely boring (and weird) if books were full of Darcie mimics. That said, it's also fun to make personal associations with characters and see elements of myself in the fiction I read, now and again. Especially important elements like my culture. With the total lack of Lipan people in fiction and nonfiction, it felt like living in the Twilight Zone, wandering through a house of mirrors with no reflection.

Thankfully, I learned about my history—my people's history—from Mom and other Lipan elders; in every ceremony, powwow, and tribal gathering, I saw my reflection. And although bullies in school tried to make me feel worthless when they war-whooped at my back and made crude jokes about my mother's Indigenous name, I had armor. Specifically, Mom strengthened my heart with stories of resilience and perseverance. Did I know that she and her family survived the floods of Hurricane Beulah, rebuilding a home in the Rio Grande Valley? Did I know that candy grew on the trees of South Texas? As a child, she'd chew the sweetness from mesquite pods. Did I know that Great-Great-Grandfather spoke to the sun in the morning, praying in Lipan when it was dangerous to speak our language? We still know that prayer because, even when our people were ruthlessly, repeatedly attacked by the US government, we did

---

5 I did once read a book claiming the Lipan Apache had gone extinct, but—in the iconic words of Mark Twain—"The report of my death was an exaggeration."

not just fight to survive; we fought to remain Lipan Apache.

She helped me feel proud. Of myself, of my culture, of the books I wanted to write.

So, amidst the difficult years of high school, I made a four-step plan to get published:

STEP ONE = keep reading, writing, and studying.
  Get in to college.
STEP TWO = join the writing program and hone my craft, making connections with agents, editors, publishers, and other writers.
STEP THREE = write a book for my college thesis.
STEP FOUR = send shiny new manuscript to publishers.

College application season was a whirl of paperwork, personal essays, and possibilities. I envisioned myself studying in Arkansas, Texas, Minnesota, New York, New Jersey, California, Illinois, and Connecticut. In terms of potential colleges, I cast a wide net, prepared—as always—for rejection. What I hadn't expected was an acceptance from Princeton University, an acceptance that came with a generous scholarship based on financial need. The vast majority of my tuition was covered, and I could pay the rest by working part-time in the architecture library.

Step one completed!

I assumed that step two would be easy. Applying to college should be more difficult than applying to the college's creative writing program, right?

You know what they say about counting chickens before they hatch. The first time I applied to Princeton's creative writing program, it rejected me.

Fortunately, I had another chance. Just needed to polish my material and retry the next semester.

They rejected me again.

That's when the harsh reality struck: there was no time for a third chance. My four-step road to publication had failed at step number two.

I had to find a different way.

And by that, I mean I switched my major from English to geoscience and continued writing fiction in my free time. Like I said, everyone's writing journey is unique. Mine happens to be full of twists, detours, and oceanographic research cruises in the Sargasso Sea.

Years passed. I studied plankton transcriptomics, moved back to Texas, earned a PhD in oceanography, and worked as a research scientist and a scientific editor. All the while, a book grew in a Word doc on my laptop. I wrote about a tough Apache nerd, Elatsoe (Ellie), with the same name as my grandmother. Ellie? She lives in a world much like ours. Well, except for the magic and monsters. Also, she can wake the ghosts of animals. Ghost mosquitoes, ghost trilobites, ghost fish. All of them with supernatural powers. One summer, Ellie's cousin is murdered by a powerful doctor named Abe Allerton. The murder's disguised as a car accident, which means Abe's seemingly in the clear. But although Ellie cannot bring her cousin back, she's determined to seek justice for her family. Ellie—with the help of her friends, family, and loyal ghost dog—investigates the crime, trying to understand why and how Abe murdered her cousin. In the process, she unravels the dark, ancient secrets of a creepy town in South Texas.

I sent the first draft of *Elatsoe* to my parents, who read every page. However, this time, my father suggested barely any edits. I'd learned a lot since first grade. He told me that *Elatsoe* was ready to send; when I need strength, I remember that moment, the pride in his eyes.

The beginning paragraphs from *Elatsoe*:

> Ellie bought the life-sized plastic skull at a garage sale (the goth neighbors were moving to Salem, and they could not fit an entire Halloween warehouse into their black van). After bringing the purchase home, she dug through her box of craft supplies and glued a pair of googly eyes in its shallow eye sockets.
>
> "I got you a new friend, Kirby!" Ellie said. "Here, boy! C'mon!" Kirby already fetched tennis balls and puppy toys. Sure, anything looked astonishing when it zipped across the room in the mouth of an invisible dog, but a floating googly skull would be extra special.

In the fall of 2018, a publisher had made an offer on *Elatsoe*. That same month, my father was diagnosed with peritoneal mesothelioma.

Mesothelioma is a horrific form of terminal cancer that's exclusively caused by exposure to asbestos. Dad was probably exposed when he was a very young man, perhaps working in the steel mill or in construction. (We'd later discover that there was asbestos in the concrete pipes he'd handled.) At the time, it was widely known that asbestos could kill. Perhaps his employers—the people responsible for exposing him and many others to the deadly substance—just hadn't cared.

I don't know. All I know is the pain that followed.

In 2019, I quit my job as a scientific editor to help care for my father. My little family supported each other as the world fell apart. My father fought to live; my mother fought alongside him. The doctors gave Dad a few months. He survived a year and a half.

In the spring of 2020, an early copy of *Elatsoe* arrived at our house. It was a gift for Dad; he held the book in his hands and said, "Beautiful," smiling. I wonder if he was thinking of the framed rejection letter and how far we'd both come. Dad, a tenured professor and the chair of the WCSU writing department, had guided the early careers of many writers, not just mine.

At the time, I was thinking about how much I loved him and how lost I'd be without his wisdom. How broken I felt, writing books about justice when there'd be no justice for my father.

The next day, I was invited on a podcast about writing. As the guest, I got to choose the episode's topic. Naturally, I'd asked my father for advice. "Dad," I said, kneeling beside his recliner, "I'm going to speak to new writers, people like your students. What would help them the most? What should I talk about?"

For a long moment, as he considered my question, we sat in silence.

Then Dad responded, "Perseverance."

It was the final lesson he taught me, a lesson he'd been teaching me for decades, although I hadn't noticed until that quiet moment. During times of hardship, I hold close my father's wisdom.

To anyone else who needs to hear it:

Persevere.

Keeping the Joy of Writing

BY JULIE C. DAO

Julie C. Dao is the critically acclaimed author of many books for teens and children, including Forest of a Thousand Lanterns *and* Broken Wish. *Her novels have earned multiple starred reviews and won recognition as Junior Library Guild Selections and Kids' Indie Next List picks. A proud Vietnamese American who was born in upstate New York, she now lives in New England.*

"Being a writer is *very* different from being an author."

Since publishing my debut novel in 2017, that lesson is one of the most important that I have learned. When you fulfill your dream of becoming an author, you leave behind the land of "I'm writing for fun, whenever I feel like it, and *hoping* it will be a book" for the realm of "I'm writing for money, contractually bound to hit my deadlines, and will *absolutely* see it be a book one day." You are an author now, and it is surreal, exhilarating . . . and utterly terrifying!

The transition starts slowly. You might still write in your pajamas and drink tea or coffee while you work. All that's changed is your Twitter bio, which has transitioned from saying "Aspiring Author" to presenting a book title, a publisher, and a release date. More people see your deal announcement and follow you on social media, and then pleas start rolling in for free copies (because who needs to make money?) and advice (because suddenly you know all the secrets of the industry!). An entry is created for *your* book on Goodreads. Amazing! (But wait, why are there already one-star reviews for a messy Word document that's still being passed between you and your editor in an endless game of Hot Potato?)

Maybe your friends and family start taking your "little hobby" more seriously, because after all, you are finally getting paid. (Or *will* get paid, since those publishing checks can sure take their sweet, sweet time!) You might hear from folks you haven't spoken to in years: former coworkers, acquaintances, high school classmates who were way too popular for you back in the day but have decided that you are now famous and hey, are you free for lunch this week, because they have an amazing story idea they want you to write and you can split the profits?

Strangers come out of the woodwork with unsolicited opinions on every word you tweet. You will be scrutinized under a public microscope like a specimen of dubious origin. Why are you writing this story? What's your identity? What's your heritage? Oh, you don't *look* like it. Did you even live in the country your book is inspired by? Do your parents speak the language? Do *you*? Why not? Why do you think you deserve to write this, then? What useful and important cultural lessons will your book teach us? What do you mean, "It's just fiction"?

And in the midst of all this, you are trying to write, revise, think about your next book, look at cover sketches, figure out a preorder campaign, order bookmarks, include everyone you know in your acknowledgments, post flattering photos and charming tweets to "engage" your audience online, and run giveaways and contests. Suddenly, you feel like you're standing in the middle of a room you've always desperately wanted to be in, but the door was locked, and now that you've found a key, you are seriously considering escaping through the window.

This is not what you wanted.

This is not what you were imagining.

When you had the time and the freedom to dream, perhaps you pictured yourself looking glamorous and confident in front of a packed bookstore, talking to all of your rapt admirers. Maybe you imagined a long signing line at a book festival, with everyone clutching your book and expressing their adoration for you, or even a glitzy movie premiere for your film adaptation. You wouldn't be alone, either, in these flights of fancy, because there is something magical and romantic and almost tantalizingly intangible about getting published. It is a deep-rooted yearning, an inexpressible hope, a far-flung goal that so many share and so few actually attain. And getting published *can* be all of those things.

But as a BIPOC, there are burdens and not-so-shiny truths to entering authorhood that your white friends won't ever have to endure, and that can be a harsh realization.

When your passion becomes your profession, it can be easy to lose your joy. You get caught in the tangles of being a public figure, of being held up as the sole representative of your entire community or ambassador for your marginalization, and of having the manuscript you love with all your heart and soul suddenly become a product, a commodity, an artifact of capitalism to which your readers will unabashedly bring their biases and baggage. And all this, while you're just trying to please your publisher and write the best book you can!

The thing about being BIPOC, though, is that we are no strangers to struggle. Many of us know intimately what it is to have to fight for this dream. I am far from being alone in having had parents who furiously tried to stamp out my artistic inclinations, devalued the happiness that writing gave me, and insisted that I go into a career that would bring me lots of guaranteed money and stability, which (to people who had to escape their countries with only the clothes on their back) are a lot more essential to survival than personal fulfillment.

Even for those of us lucky enough to have supportive families, the struggle is real when it comes time to try to get traditionally published. In the past few years, it seems that every agent and publisher has been crying out for "diverse stories" and "diverse voices," which would *appear* to be encouraging until the rejections come pouring in, citing an inability to connect, a worry that the book is too "niche" and will not have mass appeal, or the lack of an educational aspect, since some people still believe that BIPOC stories must center and educate white readers in order to be of any value. And maybe when the book finally does get acquired, the author now has the responsibility of explaining to, justifying to, and placating an all-white publishing team who may not understand their choices, and who may have a completely different idea for editing and marketing the book.

BIPOC authors know, all too well, what it is to be bled of joy.

And yet joy is integral to this career. Joy is what got us here in the first place. That breathless thrill, almost like falling in love, when you wake up excited to write. The sensation of leaving your body behind in your office chair in order to enter the action with your characters. The delightful anticipation of not knowing what's going to happen next. A lightning-strike idea that hits you in the shower. (By the way, what is it about the shower that encourages productivity? I should really thank mine in my acknowledgments.) Think about how many people in the world want to write a book, yet we are the only ones who actually make the time to do so—often carving out stolen slivers of it from long weary days—all because of *joy*.

So it follows that *staying* joyful is absolutely vital. Joy is the warm blanket you wrap yourself in when you realize, at the end of the day, that none of the other stuff matters. What got you through the door, what kept you going on this tough journey, and what makes you more *you* than anything else ever has, is what counts. When you adjust the knob on the radio and tune out all of the other voices, frustrations, microaggressions, unsolicited criticism, and so on, the only frequency you will hear is that magic you found when you first wrote the beginning of a story.

So how do you keep the joy, exactly?

Well, like I said, I've only been writing professionally for a few years and I'm still figuring it out myself. But I have picked up on a few things that are helping me as I continue to navigate these sometimes choppy publishing waters:

1) **Social media breaks are a good idea.** I know that social

media can be a contentious topic for many in the industry, and I am not here to present my opinions on whether it is useful to book sales or not. But if you are an author with a presence on Twitter, Instagram, TikTok, Facebook, or any of those platforms that many of us utilize to connect and share news with our readers, taking occasional breaks can genuinely help bring back the joy.

Social media makes it easy to compare yourself to others online and come up short. In fact, it's almost impossible *not* to. You might see peers going to book festivals that never invite you, sharing extravagant marketing that you do not receive, or collecting awards and starred trade reviews and bestseller lists that have always eluded you. Even productivity can be a source of comparison. Maybe someone you debuted with now has ten published books to your one, or a colleague wrote five thousand words in one afternoon and you haven't done half that much all month.

The online space can be a wonderful tool for networking and staying in touch. But every so often, even if it's just for one night a week, it can be helpful to unplug. Turn off your Wi-Fi, delete Twitter from your phone, or shut your electronics away in a drawer. Let your brain recharge and give yourself the grace of not feeling pressured to post, keep up with news, or stay in constant contact. Spend in-person time with loved ones, do some writing or enjoy a different hobby, and remind yourself that there is an entire world outside of publishing. I have a feeling that you will find it so restful, you'll end up taking many more breaks in the future.

2) **Talk to someone about how you're feeling.** If you can't

find your joy anymore, reach out to somebody. Writing is a solitary endeavor and everyone needs a boost sometimes. You could ask your agent or editor for a pep talk, if your relationship with them is strong and you feel comfortable doing so. They will be happy to remind you that you are talented and deserving, and there is no one you can trust more to say so because they voluntarily chose—out of a towering pile of manuscripts and pitches and projects—to work with *you*.

Find one trusted publishing friend and one trusted non-publishing friend. The publishing friend will understand what you're going through, and they might have insights to share while they commiserate with you. The non-publishing friend will remind you that publishing is a small and claustrophobic world, that most regular people have *no* clue who insert-scathing-trade-reviewer-here is and will never even see that horrible review on Goodreads, and that the fact that you wrote and published a book is a pretty darn rare and exceptional accomplishment.

3) **Take a break from the writing itself.** I know this can feel counterproductive, especially when you have deadlines to meet and may not get paid until you turn in a draft. But you know what else is counterproductive? Sitting down every day and feeling miserable as you stare at your manuscript, unable to remember what you loved about it.

As I said before, when writing becomes your job, it's easy to forget the joy you once found in it. Now there are people waiting; now there are readers with very loud opinions; now there are a million other responsibilities you didn't expect;

now there is the pressure to create. When that happens, try to put your manuscript somewhere safe and back away.

Even if you are on a tight deadline, allow yourself just a small amount of time—half a day, a whole evening, or a couple of hours—in which you do not even have to think about your book. Don't tell yourself, "I can keep brainstorming away from my desk and that way I won't waste time," because that's not you taking a break. That's you still working.

And by the way, breaks are never, ever a waste of time. Let me tell you, it took me forever to learn that. So many of us are raised to be overachievers, to excel and succeed so that we can prove our right to belong and exist.

In every field, in every industry, we have to work so much harder than our white counterparts, so it sometimes seems like rest is taboo. Like it's forbidden or shameful.

But when I have a terrible writing slump—which comes from time to time, and the worst of which have lasted months—the only surefire cure is to take time away, and I always end up feeling happier and more productive when I come back. Sometimes, on my breaks, I will find myself missing my book and thinking about it. And that's me remembering what I love about this story and this craft and this career. That's the joy seeping back in.

4) **Explore different forms of creativity.** Sometimes, you just need to remember why you love storytelling, and another type of art might help jog your memory. Many writers have other creative hobbies like knitting, painting, pottery, and more. If you enjoy a craft, you could try to make

Writing in Color

something related to your book. You could crochet a sweater or sculpt jewelry that a character might wear, make drawings or even a map of your world (which could be a cool item for giveaways later on!), cook or bake something delicious inspired by the book, or write a song or film a trailer about your story.

If crafts aren't your thing, you could put together a storyboard with pinned photos of actors who look like your characters or make a playlist of songs that remind you of the story. You could watch the film that inspired you, or marathon that TV show that always gets you excited to write, or read a book by someone you admire. There are lots of ways to reimmerse yourself in creativity and get yourself feeling excited and joyful about it again.

It's too easy to lose sight of the craft when you become an author and get slammed with the business side of publishing, so anything that grounds you and puts you back in touch with the roots of creativity and storytelling can help in a big way.

5) **Mentor another writer.** Giving your time and experience can be incredibly rewarding, and there are so many opportunities to do so. I participated in a well-known online writing contest that I was once mentored in myself, and it felt like coming full circle to be able to guide two new writers through the initial stages of publishing myself. When they got their agents and book deals, I felt every bit as ecstatic as I did when I got my own.

Passing on your knowledge is a lovely way to connect with newer authors, especially BIPOC, and you also get to relive the optimism and thrill of someone bravely putting their work into the world. You could look for teaching opportunities in your community—maybe a local college or high school would appreciate having a writer come in and talk, or a library is looking for a workshop speaker. You could also offer a blog post or send out a newsletter about the process, or host an informal Q and A for anyone interested on your social media. So many people are eager to learn more about how to write and traditionally publish a book!

6) **Collect your happy moments.** Everyone has a different preference for how to preserve joyful memories. I have an author friend who likes to write down her happy moments on scraps of paper and put them into a glass jar, which she pulls out whenever she needs a boost. Another friend has a Polaroid camera that she's used to capture fun memories at book festivals and events, and gathers them in a photo album of her publishing highlights.

As for me, it's journaling. I've kept a diary almost every year since I was ten, and I have one that's dedicated to the happiest memories of my publishing career. I've written down snippets like "Saw someone buying my debut without knowing I was there!" or "Met my editor for the first time!" or "Signed my book for an author hero of mine!" I've printed out photos of my first signing line, my first copy seen in a bookstore, my first time autographing a book, and my first time speaking in front of an audience. I've taped in scraps of badges from festivals, school visits, plane tickets, art that young readers have sent to me, and even pieces of emails and letters that I find encouraging and heartwarming and, most of all, remind me why I write.

If you're like me, you may find it all too simple to focus on the negative things, like that awful review you got tagged in three years ago, or that time a reader mistook you for the one other BIPOC at a festival, or even rejections for the next book you're trying to sell. With all of this noise in your head, you might forget that there are so many wonderful things that have happened too. In fact, they very likely outnumber the bad ones!

So gather them in one place, and when you feel like your joy is draining away, pull out those happy memories and soak them in. All you need is a reminder that there are people out there who believe in you, who want to help amplify your voice, and who want to read more stories from you, because I truly believe that every single book finds the reader who needs it.

The transition from being a writer to an author can be fraught for anyone, but especially BIPOC. Holding on to your joy doesn't mean ignoring the hurdles, difficulties, and heartbreaks we face. We should acknowledge those, speak out to help dismantle these painful experiences for newer writers, and share what we have been through in order to help others. It has always been at the forefront of my mind to be transparent so that people coming up behind me will have the best opportunity to shine and succeed, because other authors did the same for me.

But, you know, joy is a form of power, too. To remember

joy is to celebrate how amazing and rare a gift it is to have been born a storyteller. To keep joy in your art is to celebrate your incredible ability to move and influence and inspire people with just your words. Being joyful is asserting your strength, your talent, and your right to share your voice with the world, because our voices are crucial. They are necessary. We belong here and we are needed, and at the end of the day—even with all of the struggles of authorhood—there is a lot of joy in remembering that.

Acknowledgments

I would like to thank Allah (swt) for the grace I have been shown all through the years. I would also like to thank my family, without whom I wouldn't be the person I am. I owe a lot to the kindness and guidance of my writing friends, specifically Judy Lin, Roselle Lim, Sabina Khan, Sarah Suk, Julie Abe, Intisar Khanani, and Ausma Z. Khan. Thank you also to Kat Cho, Axie Oh, and Karuna Riazi, with whom I conceived the idea of this anthology in a Slack chat years ago. Thank you to my nonwriter friends who have shown me nothing but patience as I talked about the same thing over and over again: Rossi, Jasdeep, Teng, Janet, Jane, and Yash. You ladies are amazing and deserve all the world.

My agent, Katelyn Detweiler, who has championed me from day one: thank you! Thank you to Melody Simpson for doing the work with me and to JL Stermer, Melody's agent, who has worked with us to make this a reality.

Thank you to everyone at Jill Grinberg Lit. for the fine work they do.

And finally, thank you, dear reader. I hope this anthology and the essays contained within it touch you in some profound way.

—Nafiza Azad

Nafiza Azad, the brainchild of this gem, thank you for inviting me to come along for this beautiful ride. Look what we did! Wow!

JL Stermer and Katelyn Detweiler, thank you so much for your negotiating and hand-holding every step of the way. I'd be lost without you!

Karen Wojtyla, Nicole Fiorica, and everyone at Margaret K. McElderry Books, thank you so much for believing in this project and getting this book into the hands of marginalized writers.

Finally, sending all of my gratitude to Mommy, Poppy, Kira, Taylor, my entire family, my critique partner group, and everyone who encouraged me along the way. Thank you.

—Melody Simpson

Writing in Color